Contents

Acknowledgements

This study, which has been supported by the Joseph Rowntree Foundation, draws on data from interviews with girls in a wide range of education settings and from professionals working with young people experiencing difficulties in schools. The authors of this report would like to thank the girls who agreed to participate in the focus group and individual interviews and also the professionals who were interviewed or who provided information.

Throughout the study, an advisory group has supported the work. Their suggestions were extremely useful in helping us to develop the research questions to be explored. We would also like to thank the group for their comments on an interim draft of this report: Susan Taylor from the Joseph Rowntree Foundation; Joan Stead, Edinburgh University; Margaret Holland, Birmingham LEA; Terry Ryall, The Guide Association; Mog Ball, freelance researcher; Barbara Rayment, Youth Access; Howard Firth, Hampshire Social Services Department; Darshan Sachdev, Barnardo's, and Julie O'Mahoney, Social Exclusion Unit.

Towards the end of the project, a small informal seminar was held to discuss the research findings and recommendations. We would like to thank those who attended: Jackie Newvell, National Children's Bureau; Carola Adams, UK Youth; Danny Conway, Milton Keynes County Council; Debi Morgan, Milton Keynes County Council; Roz Dickson, Goldsmiths' College; and Caroline Howarth, Nottingham Trent University.

Thanks also go to Peter Kenway and Guy Palmer from the New Policy Institute and Samantha Keenan and Rob Watling in the Centre for Citizenship Studies in Education, University of Leicester, for their support and contributions in helping us to refine our thinking on the issues emerging from the research. We are particularly grateful to Susan Taylor from the Joseph Rowntree Foundation for her input and support throughout the study.

The Joseph Rowntree Foundation has supported this project as part of its programme of research and innovative development projects, which it hopes will be of value to policy-makers, practitioners and service users. The facts presented and views expressed in this report, however, are those of the authors and not necessarily those of the Foundation or the National Children's Bureau.

Audrey Osler, Cathy Street, Marie Lall and Kerry Vincent
New Policy Institute and Centre for Citizenship Studies in Education,
University of Leicester

June 2001

Centre for Citizenship
Studies in Education

Acronyms and abbreviations

ASDAN	Award Scheme Development and Accreditation Network
BSP	Behaviour Support Plan
CAMHS	Child and Adolescent Mental Health Services
DfEE	Department for Education and Employment, now known as DfES
DfES	Department for Education and Skills
DoH	Department of Health
EAZ	Education Action Zone
EBD	Emotional and Behavioural Difficulties
EDP	Education Development Plan
FE	Further Education
GCSE	General Certificate of Secondary Education
GNVQ	General National Vocational Qualification
HAZ	Health Action Zone
ICD-10	International Classification of Diseases
ICT	Information and Communication Technology
IEP	Individual Education Plan
IT	Information Technology
LEA	Local Education Authority
LSC	Learning and Skills Council

NOF	New Opportunities Funding
NVQ	National Vocational Qualification
Ofsted	Office for Standards in Education
OPN	Open College Network
PEP	Personal Education Plan
PRU	Pupil Referral Unit
QP	Quality Protects
SEN	Special Educational Needs
SEU	Standards and Effectiveness Unit
SRB	Single Regeneration Budget
TEC	Training and Enterprise Council (TECs were replaced in 2001 by LSCs)
YOT	Youth Offending Team

Executive summary

The development of good practice to combat school exclusion and truancy on a widespread basis remains an erratic process within LEAs, schools and communities.

(The Children's Society, 1999)

This report

In recent years, a strongly upward trend in the numbers of children and young people being excluded from school, both on a fixed-term and a permanent basis, has caused widespread concern. The Government recognises the links between exclusion from school and later social exclusion and this is reflected in educational policy statements and guidance (for example DfEE 1999a, DfEE 2000c and Social Exclusion Unit, 2001). Raising educational achievement and reducing truancy are key elements in the Government's strategy to address social exclusion. As a result of young people missing out on some of the crucial experience of education, they may be left alienated from society with poor future employment and life prospects. For these reasons, promoting school inclusion and reducing exclusions has been on the Government's policy agenda, with the spotlight being placed on the performance of schools and on the ability of teachers to support pupils who may be disaffected or disadvantaged in some way.

Research commissioned by the Home Office and Cabinet Office notes that:

at first glance young women appear to have benefited most from changes in education over recent years. They appear to be outperforming boys at both GCSE and A level and are more likely to enter higher education … As a result, concern has recently shifted towards male 'underachievement' and upon the need to address the imbalance …

(Dennison and Coleman, 2000)

This disparity is perhaps most marked in relation to the issue of exclusion from school where most attention has been focused on boys who form the vast majority in the official exclusion figures. Nationally, girls comprise just 17 per cent of permanent exclusions (DfEE, 2000a). As a consequence, girls have been largely overlooked in school exclusion prevention strategies and research. This is despite statistics for 1998–9 revealing that around 1,800 girls were permanently excluded from school (DfEE, 2000a), with numbers of 'hidden' (not officially recorded) exclusions, either fixed-period or on an informal basis, increasing this number considerably (Osler and Hill, 1999).

It is for this reason that our study focuses on girls aged 13 to 16 years. The study is not simply concerned with the prevention of exclusion, but considers the broader question of disaffection amongst girls in school, which may ultimately result in exclusion of some form. The underlying thesis is that exclusion from school needs to be seen as a symptom of wider concerns. For this reason, the study also examines the support needs of girls.

Aims and objectives

This in-depth qualitative study focuses on six areas in England. It has two key perspectives – a provider focus and a service recipient focus. The overall aim has been to enhance the understanding amongst relevant provider agencies and staff working with young people in education of the difficulties and potential causes of disaffection among school-age girls. One goal is to enable the development of more effective support strategies for girls, including those from minority ethnic groups.

Giving a voice to girls about their experiences in school, their views on school exclusion and the sorts of support they would find useful, has been of paramount importance in undertaking the research. This reflects the principle outlined in the UN Convention on the Rights of the Child, that young people should be consulted about decisions that affect them. It also attempts to address the 'missing voice' of young people that has been highlighted in other research (Pomeroy, 2000; Morris and others, 1999; Lloyd and O'Regan, 1999).

Research findings

A central feature of this report is that it draws on girls' own perceptions of school life and of the use of exclusion in its various forms, both official and unofficial. Data from interviews with girls and with a wide range of service providers, drawn from education, health, social services and voluntary sector agencies, reveals a complex picture of concerns about young women.

Many of the difficulties experienced by girls in school are of a hidden nature and may lead to self-exclusion or unofficial exclusion. Exclusion can be the result of disciplinary procedures, but it can also occur through feelings of isolation, disaffection, unresolved personal, family or emotional problems, bullying, withdrawal or truancy. These experiences may be as significant as formal disciplinary exclusion processes if they deny or restrict an individual's access to education and lead to a more general social exclusion. They are not reported in official statistics. These problems are compounded by a lack of quantitative data about girls in general. This situation therefore has serious consequences in terms of resource allocation and planning of service provision.

Key study themes

Girls are not a priority in schools' thinking about the problems of behaviour management and school exclusion. Throughout the study, a typical response was that girls were 'not a problem'. Such a viewpoint was also evident in many LEAs. Only by exploring a little deeper did widespread concerns start to emerge. However, even then, these were often over-shadowed by the difficulties of managing the much greater numbers of boys presenting overtly challenging behaviour.

The 'invisibility' of girls' difficulties has serious consequences in terms of their ability to access help. Since the problem of exclusion amongst girls is seen as so small in comparison to boys, resources are targeted on the latter. This may be exacerbated by a link between criminality and boys' exclusion from school. It may also be the result of the widespread perception that girls are doing well academically in school in comparison to boys. It is not only a lack of resources targeted at girls which constitutes a barrier to them accessing help – the nature of what is on offer and girls' own responses when in difficulty can also result in them not receiving help.

The nature of help on offer assumes that provision is equally available for both boys and girls. The findings of this study challenge this assumption. Whilst the research identifies a diverse range of strategies to promote school inclusion, including greater use of the FE sector, the provision is largely dominated by boys. As a consequence, not only do many girls feel unwilling to take up the help but many providers do not refer girls since they feel that the provision will be inappropriate given the gender imbalance.

This results in further male over-representation and makes it even more unlikely that girls will access support.

Girls' lack of responsiveness to sources of help plays into this complicated cycle still further, with a widespread view among professionals that a number of girls are defensive, resistant to help and tend to adopt coping strategies which involve a sense of 'escape' or 'withdrawal'.

Identification of girls' needs and the subsequent provision of services are compartmentalised. This results in needs being met by separate agencies without the necessary links being made. This applies particularly to girls who are pregnant or who have other health or childcare needs. Poor coordination of services is a major concern and can leave girls at risk of no one assuming responsibility for their support.

The use of truancy, self-exclusion and internal exclusion were reported by many of the girls in our sample. Some girls suggested that truancy is a sensible way of dealing with difficulties in school. Such unofficial forms of exclusion mean that official statistics are likely to underestimate the amount of school being missed by girls. This raises concerns about the amount of time that girls are missing from school and their lack of a right of appeal when such exclusions take place.

Gender appears to be an important influence on decisions formally to exclude a young person. Many of the girls in the study expressed the view that the use of exclusion appears arbitrary and lacks consistency. Some suggested that girls could 'get away with more' than their male peers, while others suggested that teachers expect boys to behave badly and were therefore stricter and more exacting in their attitudes towards girls who misbehaved. Professionals also reported these differences in the way boys and girls are disciplined.

Bullying is a serious problem and appears to be a significant factor contributing to girls' decisions to self-exclude. Racial harassment and bullying also occur among girls. Gender differences in the way that bullying is perpetrated and experienced mean that bullying amongst girls is not easily recognised. The verbal and psychological bullying more commonly engaged in by girls is more readily overlooked by school authorities than the physical bullying more typically engaged in by boys. As a result, there is often an institutional failure to tackle bullying among girls effectively. Failure to address racial harassment may result in physical retaliation leading to disciplinary exclusion of the victim. Whilst girls highlight bullying as a serious issue facing them in school, the matter is given a lower priority by the professionals who were interviewed.

Rethinking exclusion. The study demonstrates a range of ways in which girls may become excluded from school, either officially or unofficially, formally or informally. Girls who have disengaged from learning may be considered excluded even when they are present in the classroom and causing no problems to teachers. Whether a pupil truants or is absent from school as a result of a disciplinary exclusion, the effects are similar. Exclusion and inclusion need to be seen as part of a continuum and an individual may move along that continuum at different points in her career.

Recommendations

In making the following recommendations, the researchers are particularly conscious of the need for early intervention strategies that seek to prevent the exclusion of girls and young women from school.

What schools can do

Schools need to consider how their pastoral support systems are meeting the specific needs of girls:

- Schools should provide support (for example, a counsellor or school nurse) that can be accessed by students on a self-referral system.
- Clear plans are needed for re-integrating pupils who have been out of school as a result of formal exclusion, truancy, pregnancy, etc.
- Policies and practices that address bullying need to acknowledge the more 'subtle' types of bullying to which girls may be particularly vulnerable.
- Schools need to address racial harassment as a specific form of bullying and to provide training and support for staff and pupils in order to address this issue.
- Schools should provide support and training to teachers to ensure that they have both the skills to identify students who are experiencing difficulties and sufficient knowledge of sources of support
- Interventions and support for individuals identified as vulnerable need to be discreet and sensitive as girls and young women are often concerned about peer reactions and reputation.
- Effective student consultation and participation procedures are critical (for example, student councils, involvement in drawing up codes of conduct, policy development, etc.) and need to be sensitive to the differing needs of girls and boys.
- Specific initiatives to support girls need to recognise differences in needs between girls related, for example, to ethnicity, sexuality, maturity and out-of-school responsibilities.

- Access to support systems, alternative curricular arrangements and other opportunities should be monitored by gender and ethnicity.

What providers of alternative education can do

The research team found that, with the exception of specific schemes to meet the needs of pregnant school-age girls and young mothers, providers tend to offer alternative education that is, in principle, open to both girls and boys. However, there appears to be very little monitoring of the students referred to alternative education schemes and most of the provision appears to have been planned with boys in mind. Providers of alternative education should therefore:

- monitor the uptake of alternatives by both gender and ethnicity;
- consider offering some schemes exclusively for girls;
- consult with user-groups of girls and young women about their particular needs;
- liaise more effectively with schools so that girls can move more easily between mainstream and alternative provision;
- ensure that provision is evaluated and results are made available to other interested parties.

What local authorities can do

The research has revealed that, with an emphasis on boys' achievement and on overcoming boys' disaffection, many professionals are overlooking the needs of girls who are excluded from school or who are vulnerable to exclusion. Local education authorities can play a key role in putting girls' needs back on the agenda:

- LEAs should provide commentaries for schools on their exclusion statistics, monitored by gender and ethnicity, which highlight girls' needs, even when they form a small proportion of those formally excluded.
- LEAs might helpfully provide a directory of services to support schools working with vulnerable young people.
- LEAs might usefully publish examples of good practice in multidisciplinary working.

What government departments can do

The Government's current emphasis on boys' achievement and boys' disaffection has led to neglect among some professionals of girls' needs. Government departments need to redress the balance, recognising the link between exclusion from school and girls' levels of education which will have an impact on their employment prospects and on their own children. Support for vulnerable girls will help to avoid future social exclusion. Government departments should therefore:

- recognise that exclusion from school, as it affects girls, is much more extensive than official statistics suggest;
- review the situation of girls excluded from school, recognising that exclusion, as a disciplinary measure, needs to be considered alongside other forms of school exclusion that can lead to social exclusion;
- address the particular needs of girls through the interdepartmental ministerial group on exclusions;
- require schools and other government-funded providers to monitor access to alternative education schemes by gender and ethnicity;
- commission research on Further Education provision for under-16s, evaluating the outcomes separately for girls and boys;
- commission further research on girls and school exclusion.

1. Introduction

Overview

This report focuses on girls and their experiences of exclusion from school. In recent years there has been a marked increase in the numbers of children and young people being excluded from school, both on a fixed-period and a permanent basis. The number of permanent exclusions rose steadily during the 1990s from around 3,000 in 1990–1 to a peak of 12,668 for the 1996–7 school year. This has caused widespread concern and has resulted in a range of government initiatives and target setting. Most attention, however, has been focused on boys who are over-represented in exclusion figures. Consequently, girls are often overlooked in research on and strategies for the prevention of school exclusions.

This study addresses this information deficit and seeks to raise awareness of the problems and challenges that may face girls in school. The research sets out to give a voice to girls and to highlight their experiences in secondary school.

The research aims to enhance the understanding, amongst relevant provider agencies and staff working with young people in education, of the difficulties and potential causes of disaffection facing secondary school girls. This will contribute to the development of more effective support strategies for girls, including those from minority ethnic groups. Particular consideration needs to be given to the needs of girls from African-Caribbean communities who are almost four times more likely to be excluded from school than white girls (Osler and Hill, 1999). Not only is the provision of effective and accessible support a key factor in any attempts to reduce the numbers of exclusions, both official and unofficial, amongst this group, it may also help a greater number of girls to achieve their potential in education.

A broad definition of exclusion

The definition of exclusion from school used in this study is deliberately broad and goes beyond the physical and formal definitions that tend to focus on school procedures and classroom management issues. When referring to exclusion from school for a disciplinary offence the Government refers to either a fixed-period exclusion or permanent exclusion. This study focuses on a range of ways in which girls may become excluded from school, either officially or unofficially, formally or informally. Girls who have disengaged themselves from learning are considered to be excluded, whether or not they have drawn attention to their needs through behavioural problems.

Similarly, those who are not attending school as a result of pregnancy, caring responsibilities or other reasons are also included, whether or not they are actually recorded as truants. This is because there is growing evidence of unofficial or informal exclusions and self-exclusions (Lloyd, 2000; Osler and others, 2000). It is our contention that individual students are not simply in one of two camps, that is to say, either excluded or included. Exclusion and inclusion should be seen as part of a continuum and an individual may move along that continuum at different points in her career.

Why we should be concerned about girls and exclusion from school

There are a number of reasons why the experiences of girls in school warrant attention. First, there is growing evidence of unofficial and informal exclusions and girls appear more vulnerable to these types of exclusion than boys. Unofficial exclusions remain largely hidden and are absent from official statistics, with one consequence being that policy fails to address the problem and therefore few resources are allocated to it. Unofficial exclusions leave parents and carers unable to appeal against the school's decision and may result in difficulties when they try to find an alternative school place (Munn and others, 2000; Osler and others, 2000).

Secondly, there is concern that the particular emotional and developmental needs of girls are not being recognised in current exclusion prevention and support strategies. Girls' needs, their experiences in schools and their aspirations for the future may differ quite significantly from those of their male peers and may result in different behaviour and problems.

Finally, there are a number of experiences, such as pregnancy and caring responsibilities, which affect girls disproportionately or exclusively and which may adversely impact on their ability to attend and achieve in school, placing them at greater risk of exclusion. In a 1997 survey, 57 per cent of young carers were female (Dearden and Becker, 1998).

Other areas of concern include the poor educational outcomes of young people looked after by local authority social services departments and the greatly increased rates of mental health problems among those children and young people (Meltzer and others, 2000; Street, 2000; Mental Health Foundation, 1999). With respect to the latter, policy has focused on reducing the high rates of suicide amongst young men. For example, in the recently introduced National Services Framework for Mental Health, this is a specified aim. Much less attention is paid to self-harm, however, which is much more common in young women and where rates are also a cause for concern (Mental Health Foundation, 1999).

Study objectives

The research has four specific objectives:

- To present the views of girls and young women, including those identified as being at risk of exclusion and those who have already experienced this sanction and the views of their parents and/or carers, with regard to the appropriateness, accessibility and the effectiveness of current sources of support.

- To gather data about the incidence of girls who have experienced the more hidden, informal or unofficial forms of school exclusion.

- To consider the corresponding views of the professionals working in this field about the needs of girls, the sources of help available and the challenges posed by multi-agency working.

- To investigate examples of LEA and inter-agency support strategies, to provide analysis of the outcomes of such interventions and to identify examples of successful working practices which other schools and LEAs might adopt.

The study also gathered data about college link courses for disaffected young people under 16. Recent years have seen an increase in the use of such provision, but with very little research or data gathering taking place in terms of what is offered, to whom and what the outcomes are for the young people involved.

Study design

The research has had three strands, namely:

Focus group and individual interviews with a total of 81 girls of secondary school age, drawn from schools and colleges in three local education authorities and three education action zones in England. In addition, 10 parents were interviewed.

Interviews with a sample of staff in each of the six areas, including headteachers, LEA and EAZ personnel and staff working within health, social services and voluntary sector agencies.

A review of relevant research and literature from government, academics and voluntary organisations working in this area.

Key research questions

Overall, the research aimed to gather information about:

■ trends in exclusion of girls from school over time and with regard to age;

■ the use of exclusions amongst girls, including the reasons for and, in particular, the incidence of unofficial exclusions and self-withdrawal from school;

■ girls' expectations and attitudes towards education and their views towards sources of help in school and school discipline;

■ gender-based differences, including staff perceptions of behaviour in school and the use of exclusion and other sanctions;

■ the existing range of support and alternative education opportunities available for young people at risk of exclusion or excluded from school and, in particular, the suitability for girls and the uptake by girls of such provision;

■ the extent to which provision meets the needs of individuals from minority ethnic communities;

■ multi-agency working;

■ re-integration strategies;

■ the access, uptake and outcomes of college link courses;

■ the access, uptake and outcomes of education programmes for pregnant schoolgirls and school-age mothers.

Further information about the selection of the six areas and data collection is given in Appendix 1.

Key statistics about girls

Girls excluded from school in 1998–9 nearly 1,800 girls were permanently excluded (DfEE, 2000a.

Girls looked after by local authorities in England Official figures for 1999–2000 show that around 26,000 girls were looked after (DoH Statistical Bulletin, 2000a).

Girls accommodated in secure units For the year ending 31 March 2001, 90 girls were accommodated in secure units in England. This figure equates to 24 per cent of the total of young people in secure accommodation (DoH Statistical Bulletin, 2001–17).

Numbers of girls on local authority child protection registers For the year ending 31 March 2000, there were 14,600 girls on child protection registers in England. This equals 49 per cent of the total number (DoH Statistical Bulletin, 2000b).

Teenage pregnancies average some 90,000 each year. It is known that girls who opt out of education early are more likely to become young mothers (Social Exclusion Unit, 1999).

Young carers Young people caring for relatives, including parents or younger siblings, were estimated to total around 60,000 in 1997. Fifty-seven per cent were girls (Dearden and Becker, 1998).

Attendance at drug treatment agencies Department of Health figures for England show that in the period 1 April–30 September 2000, there were 1,452 female users aged under 19 starting treatment programmes (DoH Statistical Bulletin, 2000c).

Suicide rates In 1996 the UK rate for young women was approximately four per 100,000 – giving a total of 154 young women who died through suicide (Dennison and Coleman, 2000).

Incidence of mental health problems Figures from a 1999 survey carried out by the Office for National Statistics revealed that based on International Classification of Diseases (ICD-10) diagnostic criteria, eight per cent of girls aged between 5–15 years had a mental disorder. In the age group 11–15 years, the figure for girls was 10 per cent. Whilst overall rates of mental health problems are higher for boys, rates of emotional disorder are higher in girls. The survey also found that children with a disorder were more likely to be absent from school (Meltzer and others, 2000).

Incidence of depression Young women are twice as likely as young men to suffer a depressive disorder (Dennison and Coleman, 2000).

Rates of deliberate self-harm Three times more young women than young men engage in self-harming behaviour (Dennison and Coleman, 2000). A recent study by National Statistics found that among young people aged 11–15 who have ever tried to harm, hurt or kill themselves, the highest rate, 3.1 per cent, was found among 13–15 year old girls (Meltzer and others, 2001).

Experience of being bullied In a recent study, 12 per cent of the girls surveyed reported that they had been severely bullied; 42 per cent reported experience of less severe bullying. These figures are similar to those of boy respondents – 13 per cent and 47 per cent respectively. Of girls reporting severe bullying, 87 per cent reported being deliberately left out by their peers and 45 per cent had experienced blackmail. Over a quarter of the girls also admitted that they had bullied other children (Katz and others, 2001).

With no qualifications Labour Force Survey figures for 2000 show that 14 per cent of girls at academic age 16 (aged 16 on 31 August 2000) have no qualifications (Labour Force Survey, Autumn 2000).

Structure of the report

The report is aimed at policy-makers in government and at those working with girls and young women. Girls' support needs are varied and may require attention from a range of professional services, including education, social work and health. There is also the need for greater 'joined up' thinking between these services.

The report has been structured so that the research findings themselves comprise the central part of the document, with each of the three main chapters focusing on a specific aspect of the research. Wherever possible, we have used the words of the girls themselves to illustrate the issues raised.

Chapters Two and Three provide the context for the study. Chapter Two provides a brief review of the literature on exclusion from school and discusses some of the prominent themes and issues. Chapter Three outlines the legal and policy contexts and presents several case studies of projects working with girls to promote school inclusion and prevent exclusion that were developed as a result of national policy initiatives. (An overview of policy initiatives is contained in Appendix Two.)

Chapter Four presents data obtained from interviews and focus groups with girls. It also summarises information from parents whose daughters have experienced difficulties in school including self-withdrawal and formal exclusion. Chapter Five presents the perspectives of professionals working with girls and young women.

Chapter Six discusses the findings of a review of FE college provision for young people under 16, education facilities for pregnant schoolgirls and special projects to promote school inclusion. A number of case studies are also presented.

In Chapter Seven, the key research findings from both the service providers and recipients are considered. This chapter makes a number of recommendations for schools, LEAs and central government to improve provision and prevent exclusions amongst young women.

2. Research on exclusion from school

> It is clear that the process of school exclusions subjects young people to what is, in effect, a double jeopardy. First, they are removed from the main institutional location for learning [the school]; secondly, they will almost certainly suffer a further decline in educational opportunities.
>
> (*House of Commons Education and Employment Select Committee, 1998*)

Media concern about behaviour in schools, often illustrated by reports of the growing number of children excluded from school, grew during the 1990s. So too did the interest of researchers in this phenomenon. Nevertheless, attention largely focused on boys' behaviour, its immediate impact on teachers, and the impact which these excluded young men might subsequently have on their communities and on society more generally. In other words, the phenomenon of school exclusion has been presented as a symptom of a more widespread problem of disaffection among teenage boys. Although researchers have acknowledged that girls are also being excluded from school, albeit in much smaller numbers, they have not been the main subject or focus of either academic studies or media reports.

The focus of previous studies

There has been extensive research into various aspects of school exclusion but very little has focussed exclusively on girls. For example, Hayden (1997) examined the growing problem of children excluded from primary school, giving particular attention to the relationship between exclusion and special educational needs. Her study made an important contribution to our understanding of the impact of the processes of exclusion on individual children, their parents and their teachers. More recent research (Hayden and Dunne, 2001) conducted on behalf of the Children's Society, reveals more sharply the experiences of families in dealing with an exclusion from school and parents' views on the underlying problems and of teacher–parent relationships. This study also includes interviews with excluded children and young people.

Towards the end of the 1990s, policy-makers began to address the roots of the problem and to highlight the costs of exclusion not only to the individuals concerned but also to society more generally. The Commission for Racial Equality, responding to the concerns of black parents that their children were much more likely to be excluded from school, commissioned two important studies: one by Parsons (1996a) which assessed the public costs to education, social services and the police; and the second by Osler (1997) which sought to identify best practice in minimising school exclusion. It is clear from this latter study that LEAs have the potential to make a difference. Indeed, recent statistics from the DfES indicate wide disparities between LEAs in the level of exclusions. The Audit Commission (1996), in addressing the issue of exclusion and the disaffection of young people, deals with the debate about the relationship between LEAs and schools.

The Social Exclusion Unit's report, *Truancy and School Exclusion* (1998), was important in emphasising the relationship between exclusion from school and general social exclusion. These links have also been made in recent research studies. Cullingford (1999), for example, studied young offenders (male and female) aged 16 to 21 and the relationship between school exclusion, home circumstances and subsequent involvement in criminal activities. Many of the young people in his study were formally excluded from school; others adopted other strategies, including truancy, which led to their effective exclusion or self-exclusion.

Research commissioned by the Joseph Rowntree Foundation has explored the ways in which various agencies, including the police, social services, health and local businesses, can work in partnership with schools to enable them to support individuals who have been excluded or who are at risk (Ball, 1998). A number of voluntary agencies publish advice on ways of maximising school inclusion (for example, Children's Society, 1999; Include, 2000) and seek to highlight the impact of exclusion on both individual children and their families (Hayden and Dunne, 2001). Other studies have examined the role of social services and other agencies in maintaining young people in school, in particular those looked after by local authorities (Normington, 1996; Vernon and Sinclair, 1998). These studies have highlighted the considerable challenges in bringing together different professional cultures, notably within social work and education.

There has also been increased interest in the health needs of school-age children, in particular, their mental health needs. In the context of an overall rise in mental health problems amongst young people (Street, 2000; Meltzer and others, 2000), a number of studies have highlighted the high incidence of mental health problems amongst young people who are excluded from school and the risks of further mental health problems which may result from exclusion (Audit Commission, 1999a; Kurtz and Thornes, 2000). Research has examined the adverse consequences for young people's mental health of bullying within schools (Salmon and others; 2000; Katz and others, 2001). A considerable body of research also focuses on how to promote children's emotional well-being and mental health in schools (Wilson, 1996; Buchanan and Hudson, 2000) and the importance of developing effective links between education and Child and Adolescent Mental Health Services (CAMHS) (Audit Commission, 1999b; Street, 2000).

A whole school approach to tackling exclusion

The Social Exclusion Unit report also acknowledged the complexity of the reasons behind school exclusion and the need for multi-agency responses. Guidelines for minimising exclusion from school, developed out of research on 'good practice' schools, have highlighted the importance of whole school approaches to policy and practices relating to such issues as behaviour management, equal opportunities and the curriculum (Osler, 1997). DfEE guidance (1999a) is also helpful in that exclusion is no longer represented as a question of behaviour and discipline, but is set within a framework which stresses the need for high quality pastoral care. Nevertheless, there is little qualitative research that enables us to understand how exclusions fit into the life of schools, how they are viewed by teachers and headteachers and the procedures that lead some pupils to permanent exclusion while others manage to remain in school or return after a fixed-period exclusion (Gillborn and Gipps, 1996). There is, however, some research which shows how young people's engagement in decision-making at school can support a more positive ethos and approach to discipline which enables schools to avoid the use of exclusion (Osler, 1997 and 2000).

There has been a tendency, both in LEA responses to the problem and in the research, to address *either* the issue of racial equality *or* that of special educational needs. As a recent report from the Department for Education and Employment points out, this means that policy responses have often been inadequate:

Analyses of the problem have tended to focus on one or another
of the groups of children judged to be vulnerable to exclusion
(specific ethnic minorities, those with statements of special
educational need) leading to strategies which fail to recognise
that, in practice, there may be considerable overlap between
these categories. If effective remedies are to be found to the
current high levels of school exclusion then researchers and
policy-makers need to develop a more comprehensive analysis.

(Osler and others, 2000)

An increase in exclusions?

In 1998–9 a total of 10,438 children were permanently excluded from school,
according to official statistics (DfEE, 2000a). There is evidence of an overall increase
in the number of exclusions across various types of schools over the past decade,
although the figures for 1998–9 and 1999–2000 show a small decrease. In the school
year 1998–9 official statistics indicate there were 1,366 permanent exclusions from
primary schools (DfEE, 2000a). Although the proportion of the primary school
population was small, these exclusions nevertheless amounted to 13 per cent of the
total number of permanently excluded pupils (DfEE, 2000a). A recent report
confirms earlier research that the official statistics may hide a significant number of
unofficial and therefore unrecorded exclusions, both permanent and fixed-term
(Osler and others, 2000).

Special schools have also seen an overall rise in the numbers of excluded pupils
during the 1990s, with nearly one fifth of special schools excluding at least one pupil
in 1997–8. Research in one metropolitan LEA noted a 'marked increase in
exclusions from special schools, particularly schools for children with emotional and
behavioural difficulties' (Osler and others, 2000). In 1997–8 the number of children
recorded as permanently excluded from special schools was 570 or 0.58 per cent of
the special school population. These special school exclusions amounted to five per
cent of all permanently excluded pupils during this period. Nevertheless, the bulk of
permanent exclusions (83 per cent) occur in secondary schools.

Who is excluded?

In addressing the question of who is excluded, we first need to remember that both
researchers and government policy-makers have tended to adopt a rather narrow

definition of school exclusion. Exclusion is usually taken to mean the process of official and recorded exclusion from school in response to a breach of the school's behavioural policy or disciplinary code. In other words, what both officials and researchers have tended to address are the exclusions that are recorded, rather than those which may go unrecorded.

Secondly, since permanent exclusions have been more thoroughly recorded and reported than fixed-period exclusions, it is the former that are usually referred to when trying to quantify exclusion from school. Permanent exclusions remain a small percentage of the total number of official exclusions, both permanent and fixed-period. Thirdly, we have evidence of unofficial exclusions by schools. It has long been recognised that official statistics on exclusion do not include 'The hidden numbers of children who have not been formally excluded but who are out of school because they have clearly been rejected by their schools' (Advisory Centre for Education, 1993). Such exclusions may be permanent, for a fixed period or even indefinite. Parents may be encouraged to find another school before a school formally excludes their child (Mayet, 1993; Gillborn, 1995) or informal exclusions may be disguised as medical problems (Stirling, 1994; Osler and Osler, in press).

Finally, as we argue in this study, it is critical that we expand our definition of exclusion to include those young people who are effectively excluded from the processes of learning, even though some of them may be in school or recorded as being in school. These include those children and young people whose needs or problems have gone unaddressed and those who may be truanting, who may or may not be recorded as absent. It is also important, when considering the needs of girls and young women, to keep in mind other factors such as ethnicity, age and special educational needs in understanding the complex process of exclusion.

Gender

Official statistics show that, for primary schools, boys are over ten times more likely to be permanently excluded than girls (Ofsted, 2000). For secondary schools, the ratio of boys to girls excluded is around four to one. As has been argued above, and as we demonstrate from our empirical research, these figures do not present the full picture. Researchers studying school exclusion in Scotland have noted how gender differences in behaviour, and the resulting differential patterns of exclusion, have largely been taken for granted by the teachers whom they interviewed (Munn and others, 2000; Lloyd, 2000). In particular, gendered patterns of exclusion may be explained by the following factors:

- girls' deviance in school may be different from boys';
- schools may have gendered models of deviance;
- schools employ different strategies with boys and girls;
- teachers respond differently in classrooms to girls and to boys;
- the ethos and culture of the school is likely to be gendered;
- commitment to equal opportunities affects how schools respond to deviance.

(Lloyd, 2000 p.261)

While girls are less vulnerable to permanent official exclusion than their male peers, their patterns of behaviour and responses to difficulties in learning or in relationships with their peers or with teachers may cause them to adopt other strategies than those which lead to formal exclusion as a disciplinary measure. Girls may be treated more leniently than their male peers for certain offences but where they display behaviour which is not considered feminine, such as physical violence, their treatment may be more harsh.

Ethnicity

An Ofsted report on exclusions from secondary school noted that:

> An increasing number of LEAs are aware of and concerned
> about the disproportionate numbers of minority ethnic pupils, in
> particular boys of Caribbean and African heritage (but
> increasingly also boys of Pakistani heritage), being excluded.
>
> *(Ofsted, 1996)*

The report also notes that the case histories of excluded Caribbean children differed markedly from their white peers and that in one case racial abuse was a factor.

The high representation of African-Caribbean pupils amongst those excluded from school raises concern about the effects of exclusion on these particular pupils and on their access to examinations. Importantly, it also raises wider questions about the quality of pastoral care experienced by other pupils of Caribbean descent (Nehaul, 1996; Wright and others, 2000). Although most attention has focused on African-Caribbean boys, we know that African-Caribbean girls are also more vulnerable to exclusion from school than their white female peers (Osler and Hill, 1999).

A second Ofsted report, *Improving Attendance and Behaviour in Schools* (Ofsted, 2001), raises a number of important issues concerning the disproportionately high levels of exclusion of black pupils. Drawing on HMI inspection evidence gathered from ten secondary schools, it observes that the reasons for the disproportionate exclusion of black pupils:

> ... are rarely clear-cut, but many black pupils who find themselves subject to disciplinary procedures perceive themselves to have been unfairly treated. Analysis of reasons for exclusion in the schools sometimes showed a difference by ethnicity. Black pupils were more likely to be excluded for what was defined by schools as 'challenging behaviour' ... The length of fixed-term exclusions varied considerably in some schools between black and white pupils for what were described as the same or similar incidents.
>
> *(Ofsted, 2001, para. 86)*

Nevertheless, the Ofsted report fails to make any recommendations that might address these apparent inequalities existing between ethnic groups.

Age

Official statistics indicate that the peak age for exclusion from school is 14 years. Exclusion is most common in Years 10 and 11, the final years of secondary school (DfEE, 2000a). Thus a significant proportion of exclusions occur after pupils have started their GCSE courses and it is often difficult for such pupils to find places in alternative schools where they can do the same options and GCSE courses.

Special Educational Needs (SEN)

There is some debate about the extent to which pupils with special educational needs (SEN) are represented amongst excluded pupils. This partly reflects problems and discrepancies in defining which pupils fall into this category. A number of researchers argue that some children are excluded when what is required is assessment and provision of special educational needs (Norwich, 1994; Parffrey, 1994). In a study of the exclusion statistics in one local education authority, the researchers observed that:

> Although official national statistics recognise the over-representation of children with SEN among those excluded from school, these statistics only count excluded pupils with a statement of special educational needs and thus record pupils with SEN as a minority (17 per cent) of all exclusions (DfEE,

1997). Analysis of the Birmingham data, which allows us to
consider all pupils on the special educational needs register,
indicates that over half of the children permanently excluded
from Birmingham schools have special educational needs.

(Osler and Hill, 1999 p.44)

Children looked after

There is evidence that children looked after by local authorities are massively over-
represented among excluded pupils (Ofsted, 1996; House of Commons Education
and Employment SelectCommittee, 1998; Social Exclusion Unit 1998) and there are
estimates that as many as 30 per cent of children in public care are out of
mainstream education through exclusion or truancy (Social Exclusion Unit, 1998).
Alongside this, the serious underachievement of children in public care has been
highlighted (DfEE 1999a; DfEE, 2000c).

Socio-economic factors

Hayden (1997) found some correlation between number of pupils having free
school meals and number of exclusions in a school, but notes that some schools in
socially disadvantaged areas have a very low level of exclusion and vice versa.
Rowbotham (1995) also found that some schools with a high level of deprivation
have a low rate of exclusion and concludes that successful behaviour management is
'a matter of ethos, policy and management'. These findings are confirmed by
research carried out on behalf of the Commission for Racial Equality (Osler, 1997).

The difference between local authorities and schools

Exclusion rates vary considerably between LEAs (Kinder and others, 1999; Osler and
others, 2000). Parsons and Howlett (1995) express the view that 'this variation is
much greater than can be explained by the socio-economic characteristics of the
area'. LEAs also vary in the degree to which they monitor exclusions by gender, age
and ethnicity, and in the amount of feedback they provide to schools, allowing them
to make comparisons with similar schools over a number of years. Schools with
similar pupil catchments show very different rates of permanent and fixed-period
exclusions (Osler, 1997; Audit Commission, 1999b). Such variations can be
explained in terms of different approaches to behaviour management and pastoral
support.

Summary

Previous research into exclusion from school has tended to define school exclusion largely in terms of official fixed period or permanent exclusion in response to a disciplinary offence. The identification of patterns and trends in the number of exclusions and the assessment of which groups are more vulnerable to exclusion have both largely been made by analysing official statistics of permanent exclusions. While ethnicity, gender, socio-economic status and special educational needs all have an impact on an individual's chance of being excluded, it seems likely from the research evidence that the biggest factor influencing whether a pupil is likely to be excluded from school is the particular school s/he attends (Ofsted, 1996; Osler and others, 2000). Nevertheless, both gender and ethnicity appear to be significant factors determining whether a particular behaviour will result in exclusion and, in the case of fixed-period exclusion, the length of the period excluded from school.

3. The legal and policy context

The legal context of school attendance, exclusion and guidance on the management of behaviour in school

Parents have the primary responsibility for ensuring that pupils of compulsory school age attend school regularly. Schools have a responsibility to monitor attendance, to make contact with parents where attendance is a concern and to ensure that they 'make clear to pupils and parents that unauthorised absence is taken seriously' (DfEE, Circular10/99).

Exclusions from school were first regulated in England and Wales by the 1986 Education Act (No. 2) and subsequent Education Acts have expanded and developed provision. Guidance and a variety of circulars have also been issued by the DfEE on managing attendance at school, the circumstances under which exclusion may be used and the procedures for re-integration.

There are three categories of exclusion which are widely recognised:

- *permanent exclusion* where a pupil is removed from a register of a school;
- *fixed-period exclusion* where a pupil is excluded for a specific period of time and is then re-admitted to the school from which they were originally excluded;
- *informal exclusion,* which may last for a few days, is not officially recorded on the pupil's file or may be shown as an authorised absence (Osler and others, 2000) and which essentially allows for a period of 'cooling off'.

In addition, this study and a number of other recent research studies have identified *internal exclusion,* which is also sometimes referred to as *isolation* or *academic removal* (Munn and others, 2000). This is where a young person may be removed from a class or subject but will not be removed from the school premises. They may instead be made to sit in the school corridor, in a room on their own or perhaps be individually supervised by a teacher in the school library.

Both permanent and fixed-term exclusions are subject to clear procedures that involve head teachers, school governors, LEAs, parents and the pupil. Circular 10/99 states that a decision to exclude a child should be taken only:

■ in response to serious breaches of a school's discipline policy; and

■ if allowing the pupil to remain in school would seriously harm the education or the welfare of the pupil or others in the school.

The guidance also stipulates that, in most cases, before excluding a child, a range of alternative strategies should be tried. These include mentoring, implementing a pastoral support programme, use of FE college and work-related programmes for older teenagers and the use of learning support units and in-school centres. It is noted, however, that 'this is not meant to prevent immediate action to protect pupils and staff, including fixed-period exclusion'. Furthermore, a permanent exclusion 'can be given for a first offence, for example, involving violence, but only when the headteacher has had further opportunity (not in the "heat of the moment") to consider the incident in question'.

The law permits headteachers to exclude a pupil for *up to 45 days* in a school year. Individual exclusions should be for the shortest time necessary. Where the exclusion consists of a single block of *more than 15 school days*, the headteacher is required to make plans to ensure that the pupil can continue their education, how the time will be used to address the pupil's problems and how re-integration will take place.

Formal exclusion processes

The exclusion process

■ Sole responsibility in considering whether to uphold or overturn the headteacher's decision to exclude now lies with the school governing body.

■ Every governing body has to establish a disciplinary committee to discharge its function in reviewing exclusions. Following the notification of an exclusion of over 15 days, the disciplinary committee should meet no earlier than the sixth school day and no later than the 15th school day. For fixed-period exclusions of between six and 15 days, the meeting has to be held between six and 50 school days after notification.

■ LEAs can exert influence through the presence of their officers at disciplinary committees, who can make representations about exclusions.

■ The duty to inform parents of the disciplinary committee's decision and its reasons (and the parents' right to appeal within 15 school days) lies with the committee itself.

Parents should be informed immediately or within one school day of the outcome of the hearing.

■ In the event of a parental appeal, LEAs must set up an independent appeal panel of three to five members. At least one member must have experience of education in the area and one must be a lay person without a background in education management or provision. Members must *not* be elected members of either the LEA or the governing body concerned, or have ever had connections with either.

LEA responsibilities towards pupils excluded from school

■ LEAs must ensure that, where possible, pupils are quickly re-integrated into mainstream schools.

■ LEAs have a duty to ensure that all pupils who are excluded for more than 15 days receive a suitable full-time education (from September 2002).

Source: Adapted from Audit Commission (1999b): Box J, p.46

The policy context of the research

Since 1997 the Labour government has introduced a number of initiatives addressing the social inclusion of children and young people (Ainscow and others, 1999). Many of these relate generally to children and families, while others are more specifically aimed at tackling youth crime or designed to promote young people's mental health. A key education policy objective is to tackle disaffection and raise standards of attainment (House of Commons Education and Employment Select Committee, 1998). A number of initiatives address pupil behaviour, truancy and exclusion. The spotlight is generally on the performance of schools and on the ability of teachers to support pupils who may be disaffected or disadvantaged in some way.

In 1998, the Social Exclusion Report, *Truancy and Social Exclusion* (Social Exclusion Unit, 1998), set out a broad framework in which exclusions are to be tackled. The most important elements of this framework are:

■ A one third reduction in the levels of both permanent and fixed-term exclusions by 2002.

■ A requirement placed on LEAs to set targets for a reduction in permanent exclusions within their Education Development Plans (EDPs).

- Guidance on exclusions which has statutory force, including the creation of new grounds of appeal and the ending of exclusions for 'minor' offences.

- A statutory obligation is now placed on LEAs to offer young people who are excluded education that is both full-time and appropriate. Each young person is required to have an Individual Education Plan (IEP) which should include a target date for re-integration.

The government has also made a clear commitment to reduce the number of teenage pregnancies as highlighted in its report *Teenage Pregnancy* (Social Exclusion Unit, 1999).

The aims are twofold:
- to reduce the rate of teenage conceptions, with the specific aim of halving the rate of conceptions among under 18s by 2010;
- to get more teenage mothers into education, training or employment, to reduce the risk of long-term social exclusion.

In 1999, the report into the police handling of the murder of Stephen Lawrence (Macpherson and others, 1999) was published. The report made a number of important recommendations relating to education and proposed that schools should monitor the self-defined ethnic identity of excluded pupils.

Key education policy development and guidance

Circular 10/99 *Social Inclusion: Pupil Support*, a DfEE guidance circular issued in collaboration with the Social Exclusion Unit, the Department of Health and the Home Office, 'brings together for the first time advice on pupil behaviour and discipline, improving attendance, the use of exclusion and on re-integration' (DfEE, 1999a).

From 1999, the Government has made available nearly £500 million over three years to assist schools in tackling discipline and behaviour problems. The Social Inclusion Pupil Support Grant is available to LEAs and is intended to target resources at programmes to reduce non-attendance and disruptive behaviour within schools. *Social Inclusion: The LEA role in pupil support* (DfEE, 1999b) provides statutory guidance for LEAs regarding the management of attendance, alternative provision and pupils at risk of exclusion.

In May 2000, joint DoH/DfEE statutory guidance was issued aimed at tackling the underachievement of young people looked after by local authorities – *Guidance on the Education of Children and Young People in Public Care* (DfEE, 2000c) and accompanying *Circular DoH HAC 2000/13*. The guidance set out a number of measures to assist local authorities in their role as substitute parents and to bring the educational attainment of looked after young people closer to that of their peers. In October 2000, a summary document was published which requires schools to designate teachers to advocate for young people in care and to liaise with other services. Every looked after young person is required to have a Personal Education Plan (PEP).

In addition to statutory guidance, special funding has been made available through the Standards Fund and Excellence in Cities initiative. Some Education Action Zones have also developed innovative plans, including the development of virtual zones supporting a number of schools spread across a wide geographic area.

Case studies

In undertaking this research, enquiries were made as to new developments in the provision of support to young people experiencing difficulties in school. A wide variety of projects were identified and it would appear that new funding mechanisms are promoting inter-agency initiatives. Several important findings emerged from this part of the research:

- Much of the new provision which has resulted from national policy initiatives has been focused on boys and, as a consequence, uptake has been predominantly by boys.
- Where provision has been targeted at girls, or girls have been actively invited to participate, the girls involved have been reported as clearly valuing and making good use of the provision on offer.

The following three examples illustrate support initiatives identified in the study which are either specifically focused on girls or where uptake by girls has been high.

Case example for Connexions

Based in Lewisham, London, this project is one of the first round of five Connexions pilot studies in England. The project is mapping provision and needs in the borough. Thirteen Personal Advisers (PAs) have started work in schools and in the community. They have been drawn from a range of backgrounds including the careers service, youth and social services, YOTs, teachers and community workers.

Self-referral is seen as one of the positive aspects of the project because it gives pupils the chance to seek support without having to go through a formal school system. However, it also means that workers are swamped with referrals and must select pupils according to greatest need and urgency. It appears that the support is highly rated by pupils. Indeed, the girls who were interviewed for this study clearly valued the targeted support they had received from their PA. One important factor for the girls was having access to an adult other than a teacher, whom they could trust. However, A PA suggested that one of the dangers of the new scheme is that vulnerable pupils could become dependent on their PA.

Case example of a multi-agency project – CAMHS (Mental Health Grant) and SRB

This York based project, which is jointly funded by CAMHS and SRB, provides support to one primary and one secondary school. The general aim is to promote a positive school ethos and to provide a range of support structures. Staffed by a multidisciplinary team drawn from various community services and including psychologists, education social workers, school nurses and youth workers, various interventions are offered. These include individual or family work, groupwork and outreach support. Senior pupils are encouraged to offer support to younger pupils who are in trouble, being bullied or need general help, via lunchtime clubs. The project also runs self-esteem clubs for seven-to-nine-year-old pupils (boys and girls) and a young women's group, which provides support and information.

A new project currently being planned is the youth enquiry service where the project team will link up with school nurses to work with young women. It is anticipated that this will be particularly useful for pregnant schoolgirls. According to the project team, work involving families has been particularly effective and parents have appreciated the ongoing support made available through this initiative. The girls-only groups, individual counselling and the focus on issues such as self-esteem and anger management have also been well received.

Case example of Education Action Zone (EAZ) funded project

The Aim High Project was set up in a Brighton school as an alternative way of managing girls with emotional and behavioural difficulties in the mainstream setting. The project lasted eight weeks and focused on supporting Year 8 girls. Participation was on a voluntary basis. Girls were asked to choose three targets and were helped by an EAZ worker and their head of year to work towards these. Teachers were informed of the targets and of the individual girl's views on the forms of teacher support that would be useful. The girls met a number of times each week after school to work on their chosen targets. They were also provided with the opportunity for work experience outside school, for example, taking care of young children and working with animals. This was viewed as helping the girls to develop generic skills that they could then use within the school environment. At the end of the project the girls were asked to make a short presentation describing what they did during it and how they thought the project had helped them. Project workers reported that some of the girls later experienced recurring difficulties in school. They attributed this partly to the short-term nature of the intervention.

4. The girls' perspectives

This chapter explores girls' perceptions of success at school, their views on exclusion and how they perceive their experiences to be different from those of their male counterparts and pupils from other ethnic groups. Particular issues of concern identified by the girls are discussed and include issues of trust, bullying and access to support. Information on the ways in which the girls reported managing some of these challenges is then presented. Significantly, and in line with other research (Reid, 1999), the data gathered and analysed strongly suggests that official statistics concerning girls' absences from school under-estimates the extent of the problem. The chapter concludes with the girls' views on how schools might be improved and with perspectives from their parents. Quotes from girls are used to illustrate key themes and issues. Pseudonyms have been used to protect their identities.

Profile of girls interviewed – main sample

A total of 81 girls participated in focus group discussions. The majority were drawn from Years 10 and 11 with most groups consisting of around six pupils. Fifty-eight of these girls were then interviewed on an individual basis. The interviews took place during the 2000–1 school year.

Ethnicity

Minority ethnic pupils	11 (19%)
White	47 (81%)

Current school placement

Mainstream school (co-educational)	42 (73%)
Pupil Referral Unit	13 (22%)
Further Education College	3 (5%)

Experience of exclusion

No exclusions	19 (33%)
Had experienced one or more forms of exclusion	39 (67%)

Type of exclusion*

Internal exclusion	20 (34%)
At least one fixed-period exclusion	17 (29%)
At least one permanent exclusion	12 (21%)
Self-exclusion (complete withdrawal from a school)	8 (14%)

Other characteristics

In public care	5 (9%)
Nursing mothers	2 (3.5%)
Had previously attended an all-girls' school	4 (7%)

* categories not mutually exclusive

Key interview themes

Success at school

In line with other research (Lloyd and O'Regan, 1999; Pomeroy, 2000) most of the girls interviewed made a clear link between school qualifications and better employment prospects and defined success at school largely in terms of good GCSE grades. Even those who had experienced significant difficulties in school wanted 'an education' and some went so far as to express regret at missing school through truancy in earlier years. Some participants also saw value in the social aspects of school and considered building and maintaining good friendships to be an important outcome of school attendance.

Perceived differences between boys and girls

The girls identified a number of ways in which they saw themselves and their school experiences to be different from those of their male counterparts. These include differences in:

- responses to authority;
- what constitutes a desirable reputation among peers;
- social relationships and inter-personal conflict;
- experiences of bullying.

Responses to authority

Many interviewees expressed the view that boys are more frequently subject to disciplinary sanctions, such as exclusion, because they tend to present a more direct challenge to authority by engaging in forms of behaviour that are more difficult to ignore, including fighting and physically or verbally aggressive behaviour. They attributed some of this behaviour to boys being more impulsive and outwardly reactive and stressed the importance to some boys of maintaining a particular image or reputation – that of an 'I don't care' attitude to schoolwork and authority. Girls, on the other hand, were perceived as less impulsive, more conformist and less frequently presenting a direct challenge to authority.

Reputation

The girls identified a number of gender differences in what constitutes a 'good' reputation. They spoke of boys having to 'prove themselves' and 'look macho' whereas for girls, whilst not letting themselves be 'pushed around', being friendly was seen as being more important. They thought that a good reputation for a boy would include:

> To have slept with loads of girls … be suspended from school … not to do homework … cheek all the teachers. They think that's good, 'cause then all their friends will be saying, 'Oh, he's good he is'.
>
> *Kylie and Nicole, Year 10, mainstream school, no exclusions*

Physical appearance was seen as very important and a point of considerable criticism from other girls. These differences relate to differences in the social construction of masculinity and femininity. There is pressure on both boys and girls to behave in accordance with gender-prescribed norms (Hey, 1997; Epstein and Johnson, 1998).

Social relationships

Girls identified the opportunities that school provides to build friendships as one of the most valued outcomes of education. Nevertheless, it seems that friendships can also be a source of great tension and conflict and friendship problems often hinder learning:

> There's distractions from a lot of my friends. If you have a fallout with someone you don't focus on the work, you're more likely to focus on your mate and trying to make up or have a go at them or something. That would be my main problem really.
>
> *Julie, Year 11, mainstream school, no exclusions*

Interviewees perceived girls as generally being more critical of each other. They also spoke of girls being more 'catty' and 'bitchy' with one another. They tend to have long drawn out verbal/emotional conflicts with each other while boys tend to resolve differences with each other more quickly through a physical fight:

> Boys are always fighting ... but it depends though ... sometimes you just see 'em like they 'ave a little row and like they're friends again the next day ... but with girls, it lasts longer. They don't speak for ages like.
>
> *Rachael, Year 11, PRU, permanently excluded*

These findings are in line with Hey's (1997) ethnographic research on social relationships between schoolgirls. For the girls in her study, 'bitching' was a major cultural practice of some groups and events such as fallouts with friends, social harassment or being socially excluded were traumatic for those involved. These processes are often invisible to classroom teachers yet they can often have a very detrimental effect on concentration and learning. Girls' friendships often tend to be closer and more intimate than those of boys and the effects of name-calling or social exclusion may therefore be more severe for girls (Stanley and Arora, 1998).

Experiences of bullying

> Bullying is the intentional abuse of power by an individual or a group with the intent and motivation to cause distress to another individual or group.
>
> *Katz and others, 2001*

Improving Attendance and Behaviour in Secondary Schools (Ofsted, 2001) notes that 'records and discussions with staff, pupils and parents suggest that girls are more involved in sustained bullying than boys, who more often resort to actual violence as opposed to threatening it'. Similarly, the Schools Health Education Unit survey (2000) found that more boys than girls report incidents of physical rather then verbal bullying but, interestingly, it is girls who report more fear of attending school because of bullying. DfEE guidance (1999a) also highlights the emotional distress that can be caused by bullying.

Without exception, the girls identified bullying as an issue for them personally or for fellow students. They reported that *any* difference is liable to be targeted including physical attributes or mannerisms, clothing, the existence of a special educational need, personal reputation or reputation of parents. Race and country of origin were also reported by interviewees to be the focus of bullying.

The girls suggested some gender-based differences in how girls typically experience bullying and in how they perceive others to respond to it. The bullying described by interviewees can be categorised as physical (for example, hitting, spitting, throwing things, slamming a door in your face, damage to property), verbal (for example, name-calling, 'slagging off') or psychological (for example, starting false rumours, whispering behind your back, 'blanking', giving nasty looks). Girls perceived themselves as more typically involved in verbal or psychological bullying. As one participant put it:

> If a boy's going to bully he'll use violence. Girls do it mentally because they're clever. They know it hurts more.
>
> *Michelle, Year 11, mainstream school, no exclusions*

Another participant suggested that, even when bullying is clearly having a detrimental effect on a pupil, schools have greater difficulty in addressing the psychological bullying which is more typically engaged in by girls:

> I was bullied at this school for three years ... and the teachers ...
> I did go to them and my parents as well ... and, like, it helped a
> bit, but they couldn't suspend 'er or nothing 'cause she hadn't
> physically touched me but to me, it wasn't about what she was
> doing physically ... she was just destroying me mentally.
>
> *Nina, Year 11, mainstream school, fixed-term excluded*

These findings are reflected in other studies. For example, the girls interviewed in a study of disruptive behaviour identified their needs as being overshadowed by the more demanding behaviour of boys and teachers not seeing or responding to the behaviours that disrupted their learning the most, such as name-calling and hurtful talk (Crozier and Anstiss, 1995).

Some girls gave examples of teachers intervening effectively to stop bullying but, more often, interviewees thought that teachers could and should do more. One difficulty is that bullying rarely occurs in front of teachers:

> A lot of it was when the teachers weren't around, you know, when
> teachers just go out of the classroom or something.
>
> *Andrea, Year 11, mainstream school, victim of bullying*

Furthermore, a number of the girls expressed reservations about disclosing bullying to teachers, parents or even friends due to fears of making it worse or because of embarrassment.

A considerable number of girls expressed the view that there is little support for victims of bullying and that the impact of bullying is under-estimated by adults. Detrimental effects on moods, sleeping and eating patterns, and the ability to concentrate were reported by some participants. This indicates the degree of stress caused by bullying:

> Whenever I got home and tried to tell somebody I just burst out in tears ... and I was so tired because I got so upset over everything in the end I was just falling asleep.
>
> *Andrea*

Bullying sometimes leads to self-exclusion:

> And I was getting called fat and everything and then ...[other pupils] they'd mostly swear at me and ... it was just stupid but it really got on my nerves so I didn't want to go.
>
> *Emma, Year 11, long-term non-attender, now at FE college*

Other research also documents withdrawal as a result of bullying (Kinder and others, 1996). This withdrawal may go largely undetected, not least because of the greater focus placed on managing the more overt challenges to school authority posed by boys, as already noted.

Verbal and physical retaliation was another response to bullying. The girls reported that this sometimes resulted in disciplinary action including formal exclusion in some cases. The next comments from a focus group show these girls' awareness of the racial bullying that underlies angry outbursts from some pupils:

> 'Cause they [minority ethnic pupils] probably get more name-calling ... they're provoked more ... and they end up fighting and that.
>
> *Various speakers, mainstream school focus group*

The girls expressed some reservations about disclosing bullying to teachers, parents or even friends. This was usually related to fears of making it worse or because of an embarrassment factor:

> The first bit of it, when you are bullied, you don't want to say anything in case it gets worse.
>
> *Nina, Year 11, mainstream school, fixed-term excludee, victim of bullying*

From the girls' reports, bullying is clearly an issue that needs further attention in some schools.

Race and ethnicity

Proportionally more black pupils than white pupils are excluded and this is true for both black boys and black girls. For example, African-Caribbean girls are nearly four times more likely to be excluded from school than their white female peers (Osler and Hill, 1999). Most girls in our study seemed unaware of this trend. Nevertheless, a number reported that some teachers respond differently to black students than to white. They suggested that such teachers are operating within racist frames of reference:

> Say there's a big group of us, like five black kids and six white kids, you can guarantee they'll pick out the black before they come to the white. They always think the black kids are bad ... have done something before the white kids have.
>
> *Karina, Year 10, white pupil, mainstream school, no exclusions*

A few interviewees suggested that the greater visibility of some pupils (in particular being 'big and black') meant that some students are viewed as more threatening to some teachers and students.

Bullying was seen as something that might be experienced differently by minority ethnic students. Both white and minority ethnic students reported observing or experiencing bullying based on ethnicity or country of origin. This appeared to be targeted more at South Asian rather than black pupils:

> I don't think there should be racism in school. There is a lot of that in school ... racism. I was bullied when I was in Year Seven. 'You eat curries' ... a lot of that ... 'you shouldn't be here, this isn't your country' and things like that ... and I didn't really like that.
>
> *Usha, Year 10, mainstream school, no exclusions*

Physical retaliation to racial bullying was reported by some pupils to have resulted in disciplinary procedures, in some cases without the underlying racial element being acknowledged or addressed.

Trust and relationships in school

The issue of trust and respect between students and teachers was a prominent interview theme. This is significant in that:

> research shows that pupils identify teacher relationships that are not based on mutual respect and trust as one of the prime reasons which influences their attitude to school … Studies have shown that bad teacher–pupil relations can be a major factor in subsequent 'bunking off' school …
>
> *(Children's Society, 1999)*

When interviewees talked about having relationship difficulties with teachers, it was usually with some rather than all teachers. Nevertheless, a considerable number of the girls interviewed showed a marked lack of trust towards teachers in general, to the extent that no matter how serious their difficulties, they would not approach a teacher with their problems.

Reasons given for lack of confidence in teachers related to privacy and confidentiality. Some feared being discussed by other teachers in the staffroom. Others expressed worries that their parents would be informed or that their difficulties would be mentioned to other pupils. For these girls, teachers were seen as not respecting their pupils and failing to take their concerns seriously.

> If teachers discuss your problems behind your back in the staffroom, they do not respect you. You have to go to teachers who have earned respect.
>
> *Anne, Year 11, mainstream school, no exclusions*

A number of respondents highlighted difficulties in relationships with some teachers. Examples were given of teachers shouting, making threats and even resorting to personal insults. Some girls felt that they or their families had been given a bad reputation, to the extent that they were always being blamed and picked out from their peers if the class was misbehaving:

> They are the good girls and we are the bad girls. They don't believe us, they believe them … we don't know why, it's just what they [teachers] say.
>
> *Carla, Year 11, mainstream school, fixed-term excludee*

In some schools, it was difficult to establish relationships with teachers because of high staff turnover:

> It is like moving house ... you are in a different place... and
> every year it feels like a different place ...
>
> *Anne, Year 11, mainstream school, no exclusions*

Use of exclusions

> The system is neither fair or logical ... you make one stupid
> mistake and they exclude you.
>
> *Anne, Year 11, mainstream school, no exclusions*

One key issue raised in relation to the use of exclusion was the apparently arbitrary
or random way in which some schools apply this sanction. Munn and others (2000)
also identified this issue. A number of girls also suggested that gender is an
important factor in deciding whether or not to exclude a pupil. Their experiences
highlight the widespread use of internal exclusion or isolation in school. Twenty of
the 58 girls (34 per cent) who participated in individual interviews reported
experiencing this type of sanction

Many respondents described a lack of consistency in relation to exclusions and
suggested that factors such as the particular teacher involved, the mood of the
teacher and teachers' perceptions of a particular student were crucial in determining
whether an incident would lead to exclusion. Reputation again emerged as an
important factor that can increase the likelihood of a young person being excluded.
A number of the respondents reported double standards and felt that they had been
blamed for the actions of others:

> If I get excluded, they build it all up, everything I do wrong and
> then they bring it all out. But with my mates, they just exclude
> them for, like, one day...
>
> *Lucy, Year 11, mainstream school, numerous fixed-term exclusions*

Participants thought that pupils with 'big mouths' and pupils who were 'naughty'
were more likely to be excluded. They tended to define 'naughty' as involving
verbally or physically loud and aggressive behaviour or ongoing non-compliance with
school rules or teacher instructions. Some girls described a strong sense of injustice
about the use of exclusion following bullying:

> It is really sticking up for yourself [which gets you excluded]...
> and then they [teachers] go back and it all gets twisted....
>
> *Tracy, Year 9, mainstream school, permanently and fixed-period excludee*

The majority of respondents thought that gender influenced exclusion decisions, although there were some contradictory views about how this influence was felt. For example, some girls expressed the view that girls could get away with more than their male peers and that teachers were more lenient towards them. On the other hand, some girls thought that teachers expected boys to behave badly and therefore were more exacting and strict in their attitudes towards girls.

The type of behaviour was also seen as important, for example:

> Most boys get excluded for their mouth and fighting but girls get excluded for different things like truanting ...
>
> *Carla, Year 11, mainstream school, internal excludee*

Some girls talked at length about their belief that the way to be noticed was to behave badly. Behaviour that receives attention is typically loud and physically or verbally aggressive or confrontational and, the girls suggested, is more likely to be exhibited by boys.

Does exclusion work?

Exclusion (permanent, fixed-term or internal) was generally viewed by the girls as an ineffective behaviour management strategy. However, some girls viewed it as necessary on occasions. For those girls who are doing well in school, the removal of those engaging in disruptive behaviour was welcomed. Parental responses to exclusion and truancy were also viewed as having an impact. Some girls thought that in their own cases, or those of their friends, exclusion was more likely to be avoided if parents and school cooperated in responding to poor behaviour. When parents and school were in conflict, they believed exclusion was more likely to occur.

Participants thought that varying rates of exclusion between schools was more to do with how the school managed and supported students than with the students themselves. Some interviewees thought that it looked good for a school to exclude pupils (conveying a tough attitude) while others thought that it looked good for a school to exclude very few pupils (conveying caring and competence).

Internal exclusion (isolation) appeared to be regularly employed in some schools as a way of managing pupils' behaviour. As already noted, around one third of the girls interviewed had been subject to this sanction:

> I haven't been sent home but I've been excluded from lessons and stuff.
>
> *Michelle, Year 11, mainstream school, no exclusions*

In some cases this appeared to be for extended periods:

> … and I was, like, outside her office for four days sitting there
> doing nothing.
>
> *Cheryl, Year 11, mainstream school, no exclusions*

It is interesting to note that many of the girls thought that this sanction was more effective as it involved a 'shame factor'.

Managing the challenges of school

A range of strategies used by girls to manage the challenges of school were described. These largely centred on verbal strategies and on various forms of self-exclusion or truancy.

Self exclusion or truancy has several problematic aspects. First, it is an indicator of need that is less visible and one that is relatively easy for a school to ignore. Second, it is a response that is likely to create additional difficulties. Absence, while providing respite from the immediate problem, increases a pupil's likelihood of experiencing difficulties with the curriculum and decreases the likelihood of forming supportive relationships with teachers and peers. Crucially, information from girls' interviews supports other research findings about the likely under-reporting of truancy/unauthorised absence in official statistics (Miller, 1995; Reid, 1999).

Verbal strategies

The use of apologies was one strategy identified by the girls as a way in which more girls than boys are able to extricate themselves from 'trouble'. Some girls thought that apologising was less frequently used by boys because they want to 'look hard' in front of their friends:

> When they [girls] put a foot wrong, well they're just, like, 'Oh,
> I'm sorry, I didn't mean to do it, I'll never do it again' but with
> boys they're just, like, 'Yeah so what?'
>
> *Anna, Year 10, PRU, permanently excluded*

Denial and crying were other coping mechanisms identified by the girls:

> Girls … they will do things and then they'll say, 'I didn't do that'.
> And more girls seem to cry when the teacher tells them off …
> I've done that and it's worked.
>
> *Louise, Year 9, mainstream school, fixed-term excludee*

When asked what effect crying might have on teachers another participant said:

> They've got softer hearts.
>
> *Nadine, Year 11, PRU, permanently excluded*

A different and possibly more developed level of verbal communication skills also appears to help some girls negotiate their way out of trouble:

> Girls ... they can talk their way out of some things ... like, they make excuses for themselves ... and boys, when they get into trouble, they just make it worse by, like, shouting at the teacher and denying what they've done.
>
> *Kylie and Nicole, Year 10, mainstream school, no exclusions*

Unauthorised absences

> She used to hate to go to school those days ... and she was missing a lot of days. She didn't do a full week for months and that's how the welfare officer got involved.
>
> *Parent of self-excluding pupil*

Self-exclusion or school avoidance was one strategy adopted by girls to manage difficulties such as antagonistic relationships with teachers, bullying by peers or difficulties managing the curriculum. Sometimes it was a way of avoiding certain or anticipated disciplinary procedures. While almost all girls in the study reported truanting for brief periods of time, a smaller but significant number reported missing extended periods of school and eight girls had ceased attending their mainstream schools altogether.

It is notable that school avoidance was rarely the first strategy adopted by the girls. Rather, a long-term pattern of sporadic non-attendance would develop over time, as other attempts to manage difficulties turned out to be unsuccessful. Absence from school often exacerbated the underlying difficulty and made it even harder to return:

> And then it's hard to come back ... you're behind with work ... can't catch up and it's easier to stay away.
>
> *Stacy, Year 11, PRU, long-term non-attender*

Some interviewees who truanted for prolonged periods made a point of attending particular lessons in a subject they liked or with a teacher they got on with.

In the case of one long-term truant, it was both feelings of not fitting in and difficulties coping with the work that led to her truancy:

> I didn't really fit in so I didn't want to go to school. Teachers wouldn't really help me with my work. It really started from there.
>
> *Stacy, Year 11, PRU, long-term non-attender*

For some interviewees, escape from situations such as these was clearly the motivating factor behind truancy. For others, truancy took place simply because the alternatives outside school seemed more appealing that day, there was pressure from friends and detection was unlikely.

Reported strategies that resulted in unrecorded absences included post-registration truancy, getting friends to lie about their whereabouts in subsequent lessons, being physically present at school but skipping particular lessons and forging notes from parents saying they were sick:

> Sometimes, I would go in and get my mark so I'd get a full attendance but after I got my mark I'd go home and I'd come back at lunchtime and get my mark and go back home.
>
> *Nadine, Year 11, PRU, permanently excluded pupil*

Faking or exaggerating illness, including the effects of menstruation and the use of emotional outbursts, were other strategies used to avoid school or get out of particular lessons. Sometimes the school nurse or matron was an unwitting collaborator in this scenario:

> They say they don't feel well and then they get sent to Matron. I done it before. Yeah. She'll just believe you and I've just sat there for, like, the whole class.
>
> *Kirsty, Year 11, mainstream school, no exclusions*

The degree to which students were able to truant appeared to be directly related to school practices. The participants who attended one school where new anti-truancy measures were implemented reported less truancy after these measures had been introduced. Measures such as CCTVs placed strategically around school grounds, random class register checks and out-of-school truancy sweeps were perceived to make detection more likely and thus reduce the frequency of certain types of truancy.

Other girls reported truanting less after being placed in alternative education. Consistent long-term school refusers who were being educated in a pupil referral unit or college reported very high attendance in their new settings. These pupils attributed their improved attendance to factors such as smaller classes, a less formal and more personalised relationship with staff, receiving more support with their schoolwork and a perception that staff care about the pupils and have a genuine interest in them. This finding supports the view expressed by some participants that many girls who truant actually want to be in education but truant as a way of avoiding the difficulties they are experiencing at school:

> I've got two friends who don't come to school sometimes 'cause they like get kind of bullied and they just go home. They don't really stay home because they want to wag ... it's because of the bullying.
>
> *Usha, Year 10, mainstream school, no exclusions*

Commenting on a fellow student who truanted because of bullying, one participant said:

> There was rumours going around about her. I don't know if they were true or not ... that she'd been sleeping around with people, stuff like that. She probably does want to be at school but she can't come because everyone's just going to take it out on her. The others just don't want to 'cause of the way they feel that day, that's all.
>
> *Fiona, Year 10, mainstream school, no exclusions*

A number of pupils drew a distinction between truanting by those who had general problems at school (for example, 'sick of it', bored, it's 'cool' to truant with friends) and those who truant because of anxiety related to a particular situation (for example, the girl who was the subject of significant harassment because of her perceived sexual activity). They thought that pupils in the former category are more likely to truant for a lesson or sometimes a whole day. The latter actually want to be at school but find it too difficult because, for them, school remains a physically or emotionally unsafe environment. They are therefore vulnerable to long periods of absence.

In summary, the adoption of a remorseful stance, crying and the use of verbal skills including denial, excuses and apologies were strategies used by many girls to manoeuvre around school disciplinary procedures. Self-exclusion was a strategy used to manage other difficulties. The degree to which girls truant or self-exclude is influenced by a range of factors including school policies on the monitoring and management of unauthorised absences and truancy. Although this was rarely the first coping mechanism employed, many of the girls in the study reported either personal experience of truancy or knowledge of other girls who truanted.

Access to in-school support and information

> They say they offer support ... that they are going to do something and then they don't do it. I don't see it as my duty to have to keep bugging them. If they know someone has a certain problem, they are supposed to help. Because sometimes you can't talk to your parents at home.
>
> *Bianca, Year 10, mainstream school, permanently excluded from one school, fixed-term exclusions in the new school*

Accessing help and information emerged as an area of concern in this study, for two quite different reasons. First, with regard to in-school sources of help, a major barrier is that most schemes are not open to self-referral. Access therefore requires the support of a teacher. This constitutes a barrier to many girls, especially when there are poor student–teacher relationships. Secondly, it would seem that a significant lack of information-sharing prevails within many schools, because school staff do not appear to know what is available in their local area or are unclear about their responsibilities in terms of truancy problems. The result is that many girls do not know where to go for help and frequently rely on their friends.

Sources of advice and support which were mentioned by interviewees include school nurses, teachers, form tutors, heads of year, parents, welfare officers/school counsellors and staff in the 'In-School' centre. In one case, the school secretary was mentioned and in another, the young person had called Childline, the confidential phone line.

There were potential difficulties with these various sources of help. Some pupils expressed the view that there was no one they could turn to. This usually related to issues of trust, confidentiality or perceived ability of that person to make a difference. Sometimes problems were 'managed' by engaging in behaviours that were ultimately unhelpful, for example, angry outbursts or truanting.

It was also notable that valued sources of help reported by interviewees were often informal sources arranged on an ad hoc basis, such as a teacher whom they could talk to during the lunch break or who made some special but informal arrangement to accommodate a particular difficulty.

Ways in which participants would like schools to be different

> I think that ... in the mainstream school, if the classes were
> smaller, the teacher would be able to cope with the classes ... and
> if they respected the pupils, they would get respect back.
>
> *Speaker in PRU focus group*

When asked about ways in which they would like schools to be different, girls' responses typically focused on better communication and teaching styles, and the importance of mutually respectful relationships between pupils and teachers. They suggested that some teachers need to try to avoid shouting, to take more time to talk to and listen to pupils and to hear both sides of a story. It was also suggested that some teachers need to develop less formal and rigid teaching styles and to be more consistent in their responses to difficult behaviour.

A range of organisational issues emerged, including the perceived desirability of smaller classes, more sources of help (for example, more places such as an 'In-School' or 'Inclusion' centre, and for schools to have school counsellors) and for more schools to have a school council (or a more effective school council) and to encourage pupil participation in the running of the school. An emphasis on preventing bullying and providing strong management support and early intervention to address some of the issues underlying behaviours of concern (for example, truancy and fighting) was also proposed. Greater parental involvement was also proposed.

Finally, having some 'girls only' activities (for example, a forum to discuss issues that relate mainly to girls, 'girls only' sports teams or a 'girls only' designated time to use the gym) was thought to be highly desirable, most especially in schools where girls are greatly outnumbered by boys.

> You know when you go into the fitness, weight rooms ... and
> some of the girls are bigger than others, they [boys] just laugh at
> their bodies and things. So I think that's one thing they should
> be separated in.
>
> *Speaker in mainstream school focus group*

Parents' perspectives

> I think to probably try and understand them [pupils] a little bit
> more. I know it's easy to say and hard to do but I think they
> [teachers] need to know … especially this day and age … about
> where children come from and their backgrounds and their
> cultures and instead of, like, blanking that out, kind of try and
> embrace it and take it on.
>
> *Parent of dual heritage pupil, fixed-term excludee, mainstream school*

The information gathered from parents of girls who were either experiencing
difficulties or had been excluded from school highlighted four key areas of concern:

- the need for improved communication by schools when difficulties arise;
- lack of provision for girls who are excluded, especially where the girl may have
  special needs;
- parents' concerns in relation to their daughters (for example, bullying) being
  taken seriously by the school;
- a lack of support for parents.

Several respondents suggest that parents are only contacted when the situation has
become serious. In their opinion, early identification of difficulties is something
with which schools struggle. They also thought that, when serious difficulties are
apparent, the overwhelming focus of the school staff is to try and remove the child
rather than look for ways to support the child in school. Accessing help from other
agencies such as Child and Adolescent Mental Health Services (CAMHS) had also
proved difficult and subject to lengthy delays.

Bullying was also raised as a major source of concern by parents, with several
interviewees indicating that the school attended by their daughter had not taken
their concerns seriously and had therefore taken little or no action to try and
remedy the situation.

Parents considered that the following would be helpful in schools:

- pupil access to a school counsellor or an adult in school who is separate from
  teaching staff;
- taking issues of bullying more seriously;
- a broader more multicultural curriculum;
- reducing the high staff turnover and use of supply teachers;
- less pressure on teachers so that they have the time to develop more personalised
  knowledge of pupils;
- greater contact between parents and teachers.

Summary

Girls perceive significant gender differences in the management of student behaviour and the use of sanctions, including exclusion. Girls' behaviours and responses to problems such as truancy and self-exclusion may be easier to overlook than the more overt and demanding behaviours of boys. This problem is likely to be exacerbated where teachers are under pressure and where there is a high staff turnover.

Lack of trust, bullying and information on sources of help are issues for a considerable number of girls. The girls report a range of strategies to manage the challenges of school but not all of these are helpful. The use of avoidance strategies and self-exclusion, for example, is problematic. Clearly, and as the girls themselves appear to recognise, the long-term consequences of the resulting loss of education is likely to outweigh any immediate benefits. The girls' reports suggest that education is valued and that they do not want to miss out through disaffection and self-exclusion.

The information provided on various forms of self-exclusion and school avoidance suggests that the official statistics concerning girls' absences from school underestimate the extent of this problem. In combination with evidence of the widespread use of internal exclusion, these findings suggest that the needs of a significant number of girls are not being adequately met within current systems. In order to achieve the Government's aim of reducing social exclusion, it will be necessary to focus on school exclusion *in all its forms* rather than the less frequent but more easily measured practice of formal permanent exclusion.

5. Professional perspectives

> The negative sanction of exclusion is often the only option left in
> schools where there are no positive possibilities. ... There have to
> be parameters and a behaviour management programme with
> rewards in place and adult role models.
>
> *Director of EAZ*

This chapter explores the key themes arising from in-depth interviews with a range
of professionals working in schools, education support services, social services and
health agencies. Fifty-five service providers across the six sample areas were
interviewed. The interviews explored the professionals' perceptions of the needs
and experiences of girls and young women at school and their views on how girls
might be better supported both in and beyond school. Where face-to-face interviews
proved difficult to obtain, they were supplemented by material from a postal
questionnaire, covering the main interview themes.

Data on permanent exclusions was collected from each area and efforts were also
made to gather statistics on fixed-period and internal exclusions, that is, where
isolation from peers was used as a sanction within school. It was not possible to
establish a statistical picture of unofficial or internal exclusions since these tend to
take place at the discretion of individual teachers, and may go unrecorded. Our
enquiries confirm that the monitoring and recording of these exclusions also varies
greatly between schools.

Key interview themes

Differences between boys and girls

The interviews with professionals raise a number of issues relating to perceived
differences in the behaviour and experiences of girls and boys at school, which may

go some way towards explaining differences in exclusion rates. These include:

- girls' greater adaptability to the academic routines of school;
- girls' greater maturity and deployment of social skills;
- teachers' different perceptions of behaviour on the basis of gender;
- gender-based differences in bullying;
- the risk of differential treatment in the use of exclusion.

The majority of teachers see the prime purpose of exclusion, particularly an internal exclusion, as a prompt means of removing a disruptive element from the classroom. The over-riding concern is generally the effect of the disruption on the processes of teaching and learning, so that the needs of the disruptive student take second place to those of the other students.

Many of the interviewees believed girls to be more willing and able to concentrate on academic tasks than their male peers. A deputy head in a mainstream school explained:

> I think that there is definitely something to do with boys being less suited to the culture of schools than girls … that schools are more friendly places for girls. And I think that some of that is to do with quite early stuff … literacy and the acquisition of language … girls start the educational process that little bit more advanced than boys.

Not only were girls perceived as being more mature than boys but they were also judged as being more aware and intentional in their behaviour and thus able to get out of trouble more easily. A member of a LEA behaviour support team suggested: 'Girls are more mature and able to manipulate the system and individuals to get through.'

There is a widespread belief among professional interviewees that girls adopt manipulative tactics in responding to adults in school. This is supported by some girls who report that they are able to 'get round' certain teachers. It raises questions about the causes of such behaviour; it appears that girls not only use manipulative techniques because they work, but also because these are the only strategies they are able to deploy. Some interviewees are also aware that the same behaviours in girls and in boys are responded to differently. For example, it was argued that, in relation to aggressive behaviour, girls are sometimes given more leeway than boys are. Whereas aggression in boys is seen as something which needs to be punished through a severe sanction such as exclusion, in girls it is sometimes seen as less 'natural'. Aggression might therefore be seen as a deep-seated problem for which a girl required help:

> I think there is an assumption that if a female is showing
> aggressive behaviours, it doesn't really fit in with the stereotype
> so they think there must really be something wrong here ... let's
> just try and sort it out. But if a boy does the same thing then
> that's it, they're out.
>
> *Educational Psychologist*

Alternatively, a girl who behaved aggressively might also be seen as more outrageous or extreme than her male counterpart, and therefore liable to experience a more severe punishment:

> Girls are greater victims of inconsistencies; there is a degree of
> intolerance but also a degree of shock and horror: they do not
> have the ability to be 'loveable rogues'.
>
> *Head of Pupil Referral Unit*

Respondents suggested that different peer expectations play a role in determining behaviour:

> Girls do better because it is more the accepted norm in school
> for girls to work hard and do their homework whereas it's not
> cool that boys do their homework and show that they are keen
> and enthusiastic.
>
> *Deputy Head, mainstream school*

This readiness of many girls to adapt or accept school cultures may allow their needs to be overlooked. One theme running through the data is the invisibility and hidden nature of girls' difficulties. Some professionals argued that the different forms of bullying that are deployed by girls and by boys leaves boys more vulnerable to formal exclusion. It is easier for teachers to identify and address the more physical forms of bullying than the more subtle, psychological ways of bullying in which a number of girls engage. Similarly, teachers may underestimate the effects on girls of difficulties in peer relationships.

> Probably the business of girls falling out ... of being friends and
> then not being friends ... certainly Year 9, Year 10 can be an
> absolute nightmare for some groups of girls ... But it isn't so
> directly confrontational with the learning culture. It's very much
> a personal problem, domestic if you like ... but it's not as
> established as 'really cool boys don't achieve'. There's not that
> direct impinging on learning within the school.
>
> *Deputy Head, mainstream school*

This deputy headteacher recognises the impact of difficulties in personal relationship difficulties on girls' lives, but not necessarily on their learning. His viewpoint supports that of many girls in this study. Teachers may only partially recognise the detrimental effects of friendship break-ups or verbal or psychological bullying on girls' concentration and learning (Crozier and Anstiss, 1995; Hey, 1997; Stanley and Arora, 1998).

Professionals tended to suggest that the lower permanent exclusion rate among girls was an outcome of fewer girls exhibiting difficult behaviour. They were unaware of any gender-based differences in the use of informal or unofficial exclusions. This perception contrasts sharply with the perceptions of the girls and young women themselves, as we have seen in the previous chapter.

Race and ethnicity

Particular issues for minority ethnic pupils identified by service providers include:
- limited access to services, particularly for Asian pupils;
- limited cultural understandings among some service providers;
- issues of race and ethnicity being minimised or overlooked (for example, in relation to bullying);
- impact of family and cultural values on the aspirations and achievements of some Asian girls.

Many service providers were aware of the disproportionate number of black pupils who are excluded. In addition, those who were involved in behaviour support services suggested that African-Caribbean girls were highly represented within their support services. This was attributed partly to inter-personal issues and teacher expectations or stereotypes. As one parent put it:

> I think some teachers might think that black kids are more aggressive. There's cultural things. Black kids can be quite loud … and sometimes that's interpreted as aggressiveness. It's about understanding the culture.
>
> *Parent, African-Caribbean*

Asian pupils generally, and Asian girls in particular, were seen as less likely to access support services. Several participants attributed this to some Asian pupils being removed from school when difficulties arose. Some participants expressed concern that family and cultural influences might limit the aspirations and educational achievements of some Asian girls. The professionals had not necessarily discussed their perceptions with the families concerned.

When services are provided for specific groups (for example, Asian girls), professionals stress the importance of recognising the differences between members of a group that might otherwise be considered homogenous:

> The fact that they were Asian girls didn't unite them. There were vast differences … different religions … and even within the same religion there were still lots of differences depending on parental and family values. For people not working with those cultures and religions, it's easy to lump them all together and make assumptions and stereotypes.
>
> *Children's Rights Officer*

Some interviewees expressed concern that issues of race and ethnicity are minimised or remain unrecognised within some schools, support services and wider communities. Racial bullying and harassment that can lead to self-exclusion was thought by some interviewees to be a major issue for some pupils.

The hidden nature of girls' problems

One theme arising from the research is the way in which the girls' needs are overlooked. This is partially explained in terms of the less visible nature of some of their problems, but it also reflects the types of strategies which girls deploy to manage problems, some of which may go unnoticed by teachers. It may be difficult to detect the stressful circumstances (for example, peer relationship difficulties) but it is also more difficult to detect that a student has opted out of learning and withdrawn, particularly if she continues to attend school regularly. Some education and social services interviewees, therefore, argue that those who come to the attention of staff reflect only the 'tip of the iceberg'. Internalised responses such as anxiety, depression, eating disorders and self-harming behaviour can be overlooked or assumed to relate to problems beyond, rather than within school.

It was suggested that teachers are often too busy with teaching and administrative duties to identify girls' problems. Faced with a range of competing pressures, many teachers focus their attention on those whose needs are overt and who present an immediate management challenge in the classroom:

> The difficulties faced by girls are due to them not acting out that
> much…. They are not 'in your face'… They are quieter, they
> tend to stop attending and they often disengage from school …
> they may only come to attention if they turn to bullying.
>
> *Deputy Head, mainstream school*

Even when teachers do recognise that a girl is in difficulties, they often do not know what to do to help her, especially if the problem is complex. Even when a student is referred to other agencies, these agencies may only respond to an aspect of the problem, thereby compartmentalising it.

Accepting help

A common perception is that many girls are reluctant to let anyone know if they are in difficulties because this makes them seem different from their peers and more vulnerable. This viewpoint was especially evident amongst the school-based staff interviewed. Staff believe that girls are protective of their privacy and determined to be independent – they do not want adults to interfere with their lives. This perception further increases the tendency not to refer girls to specialist sources of support.

The complexity of girls' difficulties

Interviewees highlighted the difficult circumstances in which some young women are living. Some may live in poverty or in violent neighbourhoods, while others may have experienced trauma while within the family. As one education welfare officer noted:

> The majority of girls who have been excluded are extremely
> vulnerable, come from disrupted family backgrounds and are in
> real crisis; some are in care, some are abused, some are pregnant
> or have had terminations; some are self-harmers or are in danger
> of some sort …

Interviewees recognised that not all those living in difficult circumstances are vulnerable to exclusion, but pointed out that these contexts need to be taken into consideration when developing preventive strategies. It was argued that girls at risk of exclusion tend to exhibit higher levels of difficult behaviour than their male peers.

Resources

The majority of our interviewees thought that resources available for in-school support and specialist projects and interventions have to be targeted at boys, since they are four times more likely to be excluded from secondary school and are believed to be more vulnerable to disaffection and under-achievement. The viewpoint that girls comprise such a small percentage of the problem of those experiencing difficulties in school was widespread.

Clearly, some girls are not referred to sources of help because their needs go unnoticed. Yet even when their needs are recognised, girls may not be referred, since teachers and other professionals believe that the provision is inappropriate, as it is both targeted at, and dominated by, boys. This can exacerbate the imbalance in the use of support provision thus making it even more difficult to refer girls to such sources of help.

As one educational psychologist noted: 'In my job I pick up girls with Statements in relation to behaviour difficulties and I think that … probably nationally the provision for those girls is poor.'

She explained that girls do not necessarily have access to the same school provision because some Emotional and Behavioural Difficulty (EBD) schools are for boys only or it is not appropriate having one or two girls among a larger group of boys. As a consequence: 'Sometimes they [girls] end up getting educated in a residential school [extra-district placement] because there is nowhere else.'

Similarly, the gender imbalance in pupil referral units was noted as problematic for some girls.

> I think the biggest issue for girls in our centres is that they are largely male environments. If we didn't have our school refusers who are predominantly girls, we would have some centres where it was almost all boys.
>
> *Member of behaviour support team*

Younger girls

> Girls' problems are different from those of boys. It is more of a hidden problem and a *younger* problem. Girls tend to stick together as a form of self support.
>
> *Deputy Head, mainstream school, our emphasis*

A number of respondents indicated that behaviour difficulties in school are occurring at an earlier age amongst girls. This issue was emphasised by interviewees from Child and Adolescent Mental Health Services (CAMHS), a number of whom also reported dealing with an increase in the numbers of young people who had self-excluded or withdrawn themselves from school, often due to difficulties with extreme anxiety or depression.

It was suggested that transition from Year 8 to 9 is a difficult period, which may culminate in exclusion from school in Year 10. In past years, such difficulties tended to emerge in Year 10 or later. This shift was thought to reflect the earlier onset of puberty now experienced by many girls and the tendency for some girls to mature at an earlier age (Madge and others, 2000). This issue of girls' maturation emerged in a connected theme, that of the relevance of the school curriculum.

Curriculum relevance

> A new learning culture means that every day there is something worth going in for and that does not need to be academic.
>
> *Director of EAZ*

Despite the perception that girls are better suited to the academic routines of school life than boys, many professionals believe there is a mismatch between the curriculum and girls' needs (see also Kinder and others, 1995 and 1996). A number of professionals interviewed believe that the curriculum becomes inappropriate as girls mature with some suggesting that girls 'outgrow' the curriculum in a way that boys do not. As a consequence, some girls become bored and detached and this process may culminate in either self-withdrawal or disruptive behaviour which then leads to exclusion by the school. Several interviewees criticised the narrow academic focus of the National Curriculum and suggested that the introduction of school performance league tables had heightened this focus. This perspective is reflected in the following observation from the head of a centre providing alternative education to mainstream school:

> It remains a school's responsibility to teach a curriculum reflecting real life. Remember the fundamental aim is to prepare children for adult life, life beyond school. Schools miss the point. They prepare for further education and do not tackle disaffection and disengagement.
>
> *Head of an alternative education centre*

Barriers to girls' achievement

Service providers identified a range of barriers, which may lead many girls to withdraw from learning, self-exclude or have a poor school attendance record. The major barriers identified are:

- limited access to educational alternatives;
- lack of specialist Emotional and Behavioural Difficulties (EBD) provision for girls;
- condoned absences and low aspirations;
- peer relationships and subtle forms of bullying;
- pregnancy;
- sexual exploitation.

A number of interviewees perceived a gender bias in the allocation of resources to students who have been excluded or who are at risk of exclusion from school. Professionals suggested that the number of places in schools that specialise in meeting the needs of pupils with emotional and behavioural difficulties is inadequate. Girls are disadvantaged in the allocation of placements because professionals are reluctant to refer girls to placements that are likely to be male-dominated and where they may be particularly vulnerable.

It was argued that girls' low self-esteem and low aspirations among many girls sometimes led them to make negative judgements about the importance of education and therefore decide to stop attending school. Some girls lack family support to continue in school and for others absence is parentally condoned:

> In some families, education isn't valued. There are quite a few young women at home … helping with the cooking and the shopping. They don't see it [education] as a way to improve their life situations.
>
> *Education welfare officer*

Professionals also believe that subtle forms of bullying were more likely to have an impact on girls than on boys, encouraging them to opt out of school.

The link between pregnancy and exclusion is complex. On the one hand, girls whose low self-esteem and low aspirations had caused them to become poor attenders are thought to be at greater risk of pregnancy. On the other hand, although the regulations state that pregnancy is not a reason for formal exclusion, pregnancy often results in unofficial exclusion or in school-condoned absence:

> The problem with pregnant girls is not formal exclusion but informal exclusion like sporadic attendance, school moves and

home tuition; pregnant girls are excluded by the back door.

Head of a Children's Society project for pregnant teenagers

A number of interviewees suggest that sexual exploitation remains a serious but hidden problem, impacting on the education of some girls. A key concern is the lack of services for those at risk of sexual exploitation. This is linked to wider societal attitudes that make it difficult to acknowledge and respond to the problem:

I think that's a real cultural problem in this country whereby we have this acceptance that men can and do pay for sex with young women. It's brushed under the carpet and ignored.

Children's rights officer

This is a serious issue which we were not able to develop in this research but which requires further investigation.

Inter-agency approaches

Service providers expressed considerable support for the principles of inter-agency working to help promote school inclusion and reduce exclusions. Some saw it as essential, given that many young people are receiving services from multiple agencies. Others pointed out that 'joined up working' is now expected but that formal relationships need to be matched by improved communication and information sharing and by strategic planning. These viewpoints echo the findings of other recent research (see for example, Kinder and others, 1998; Vernon and Sinclair, 1998). Several participants emphasised the importance of ensuring that young people are supported to participate in any inter-agency initiative where decisions will affect them. As a youth worker said: 'For this to work well, it seems to me to be critical that you have the participation of young people.'

There was considerable variation in the degree to which inter-agency work was taking place in the areas and agencies within our sample. It generally appears to take one of three forms:

- strategic planning initiatives;
- general liaison: information exchange, seeking or offering advice;
- case conferences, focusing on specific individuals.

In general, inter-agency working is best established within local education authorities. By contrast, formal links with health services were reported to be less common, while joint approaches between education professionals and the youth justice system, through youth offending teams, appear to be at an early stage.

In one LEA, having children's services and education under one directorate was not seen to have resulted in better working relationships – the management structure has changed but the creation of a shared culture remains undeveloped. Individuals within a multidisciplinary team can become professionally isolated unless good links are maintained with the parent organisation.

Advantages

Service providers identified a number of ways in which inter-agency approaches promote effective outcomes:

- improved communication and information sharing;
- multiple perspectives and a more holistic and balanced view of a 'problem';
- reduction in feelings of professional isolation;
- sharing of skills;
- efficient use of resources and cost sharing.

One model that was reported to be successful was a secondary school where there were termly meetings involving LEA agencies, the school nurse and pastoral support teacher:

> It was hard to organise but enormously useful. It helped us to identify some pupils who had been referred to the wrong agency … and others who we all were involved with but didn't realise … and others with no one but who could really use some support.
>
> *Educational psychologist*

Such arrangements can enable greater networking, which in turn enable professionals to be more effective in their daily work, as this educational psychologist points out: 'You know who to phone. You know who the 'at risk' families and pupils are and what other agencies are doing to support them.'

Challenges

Some challenges and tensions in inter-agency work include:

- different organisational and professional cultures and ways of viewing young people;
- defining roles, responsibilities and objectives;
- agreeing priorities and agendas;
- resolving resource issues.

Since each organisation and profession has established objectives and patterns of working, professionals need to be flexible and creative in order for inter-agency work to achieve its primary objective, that is, to enable services to meet the best interests of the child:

> There is this assumption when you get inter-agency meetings, it is a good thing ... because everyone is combined in the interests of the child. But the reality is that people have different agendas and different resourcing needs.
>
> *LEA behaviour support service*

Interviewees pointed out that inter-agency work can lead to practical difficulties, such as delays while meetings are set up, which may not be in the best interests of the young person. Some also identified a professional hierarchy, where certain services may carry more influence:

> Certain services are seen to have a greater weight and a greater knowledge and a greater understanding and experience. It's usually the medical services. If a GP has diagnosed a certain condition, then the school is not willing to listen when you tell them that your observations do not support that [viewpoint].
>
> *Educational Psychologist*

Summary

Like the girls who were interviewed, service providers perceived some gender-based differences in how schools are typically experienced. Perceived differences such as girls' greater adaptability to the academic routines of school, more conscious use of social skills and different teacher perceptions of similar behaviour based on gender, were viewed as contributing to the lower permanent exclusion rates of girls. There is also a perception that the type of strategy typically employed by girls to manage problems (for example, self-exclusion) means that their difficulties are overlooked. Accessing appropriate support can be problematic. The view that in-school support is targeted mainly at boys adds weight to the view expressed by girls about the difficulties they face in accessing support.

Service providers recognise that there are a number of factors that serve to limit the chances of some girls succeeding at school and they perceive difficulties occurring at an earlier age than in the past. Their identification of problems largely coincides with the perceptions of the girls in this study. Nevertheless, girls' concerns about bullying and the links they make between bullying and exclusion from school were not recognised as being particularly significant among the service providers.

Professionals recognise the importance of inter-agency work in tackling school exclusion and the wider problem of social exclusion, but are still encountering some challenges in this mode of working.

6. Support strategies and special projects to promote school inclusion

The research team examined the range of provision available across the country for girls who are experiencing difficulties in school.

The following areas of support were considered:

- the use of further education colleges in providing education for disaffected under-16s;
- education facilities for pregnant schoolgirls;
- school and community-based provision of specialist therapeutic help, provided either individually or on a group basis.

Wherever possible, projects aimed at specific groups of young people known to be at particular risk of exclusion from school were identified. Similarly, attempts were made to identify projects designed to meet the needs of young people from minority ethnic communities.

The case studies presented in this chapter illustrate that there has been a recent proliferation of different approaches to working with disaffected young people and those experiencing difficulties in school. There is, however, considerable local and regional variation in the availability of support schemes, with minimal monitoring of access. A striking feature is the high uptake of many of these schemes. Where projects address the specific needs of girls, there is considerable demand. This challenges the perception of some professionals noted in the previous chapter that girls are reluctant to accept help. The evidence from this study suggests that girls' access to key resources and provision nevertheless remains limited.

Key findings

- *The use of the further education (FE) sector* for under-16s is increasing considerably. Considerable variation exists between colleges in terms of what is offered and how this is funded and between LEAs in terms of referral criteria and the management of college/school links.

■ *Much of the under-16 provision offered by the FE sector is dominated by boys.* Many of the vocational course options currently available appear to be better suited to boys' interests. It is not clear whether this is by design or default. Either way, the result is that girls are less likely to want to attend or will not be referred because the provision is thought to be inappropriate. Enquiries made during this study suggest that there is little systematic gathering of data about course access or student retention and outcomes. There are concerns that some young people are being placed in the FE sector simply as a means of removing them from school.

■ *The review of facilities for pregnant schoolgirls* has revealed a wide variation in provision, with some units operating on a full-time basis and others offering only a limited number of hours each week. The availability of crèche and childcare facilities is very uneven. More systematic monitoring of provision is therefore needed.

■ *Special projects to promote school inclusion and prevent exclusion* focus largely on the primary sector and again are dominated by boys. This makes referral and uptake by girls problematic. The nature of support varies widely, with mentoring, either on an individual or group basis, appearing most common.

■ *Girls-only schemes* are in high demand. Girls value the opportunity to talk about personal/sensitive issues that they may feel less comfortable raising in the company of boys. Other benefits of such provision are enhancement of self-esteem and improved communication skills.

■ *Voluntary sector projects*, although often innovative, have short-term funding and may lack sustainability.

Review of FE college link courses for disaffected under-16s

Many colleges offer some sort of provision for disaffected under-16s but until now little was known about what is offered (Audit Commission, 1999b). The study aimed to gather information about the range of partnerships between colleges and their local secondary schools and LEAs. Data was sought on participants and outcomes. Information was gathered from 20 colleges across England (six in London boroughs, six in metropolitan areas and eight in other areas). Telephone interviews were conducted with the staff member responsible for the management or coordination of under-16 link programmes.

Range of provision and programme components

Information provided by interviewees about course numbers showed that FE colleges are increasingly being used to support the education of disaffected under-16s. Some interviewees attributed this to changes such as allowing disapplication of some students from the National Curriculum and more flexible funding arrangements. Provision ranged from very informal arrangements involving a small number of students (as few as six) to more formal and structured programmes that cater for larger numbers (as many as 130). Some programmes work with these youngsters as a discrete group while others integrate the students into existing courses. Some cater for both Year 10 and Year 11 pupils while others are exclusively for Year 11 pupils. There are programmes designed for specific groups (for example, permanently excluded pupils) and some for a broader range of pupils who are not participating in mainstream education (for example, pregnant teenagers, young mothers, school refusers/phobics). Other programmes are for students who are enrolled in mainstream schools but who are viewed as 'disaffected' or 'at risk'.

Over two-thirds of the programmes examined were full time college placements, while others were part time. Some pupils attend both their mainstream school and college on a part time basis thus making up a full time programme. For a minority of students, the part time college placement is their only education. Reported programme components included curriculum-based work (for example, mathematics, English), basic skills (for example, numeracy, literacy), key skills and life skills, information technology (IT), vocational training and work experience. Achievement outcomes in most cases included externally recognised accreditations including GCSEs, NVQs, GNVQs, ASDAN Awards, City and Guilds Awards, and Open College Network (OCN) accreditation.

Access

Access arrangements to these programmes vary. In some cases, access is negotiated directly with the school. More often, it is by arrangement with the LEA or jointly with the LEA and school. In some areas there is a LEA-led multi-agency panel that manages alternative educational arrangements for disaffected pupils. Interestingly, while there is clearly support for the use of FE as an educational alternative for disaffected pupils, concern was also expressed by some service providers about the inappropriate removal of disruptive pupils from school rolls or, as some put it, 'exclusion by the back door'.

Funding arrangements

In many cases, the LEAs or schools themselves are directly or jointly funding college placements. Funding arrangements vary considerably. They include funding from the Training and Enterprise Council (from 2001, the Learning and Skills Council), the Chamber of Commerce, Construction Boards and Single Regeneration Budget funds (see Appendix Two). Funds allocated to schools by the DfES, such as the Pupil Retention Grant, were also reported to support FE.

Data collection and monitoring

Pupil attendance and achievement were generally recorded and were fed back to schools or LEAs, often via termly reports. In many cases, information about future placement of pupils was also recorded. While some examples were found of systematic data gathering, formal monitoring by gender and ethnicity, in relation to course access, outcomes and retention, was extremely limited. This finding is consistent with an Audit Commission study (1999b) that found that few authorities accurately measure the cost or outcomes of alternative provision. This means that it is difficult to draw conclusions about the cost effectiveness and longer-term value of such programmes. This issue is one that warrants further attention, particularly given the increasing numbers of pupils accessing such provision.

Issues for girls

Most interviewees were able to provide an estimated figure on the gender make-up of their under-16 provision, even where monitoring by gender was not taking place. This ranged from zero to 50 per cent. In the majority of cases, interviewees reported that the number of boys accessing programmes far outweighed the number of girls. This is likely to be related to the way in which schools typically identify 'at risk' pupils (see Chapter Four). It is also possible that the limited number of girls referred and the limited vocational options available at particular colleges influence the perceived appropriateness of FE courses by referring bodies and girls themselves.

Many interviewees indicated that the vocational course choices made by both male and female students were often gender-stereotyped. They saw this as particularly problematic for girls because of the limited course options addressing girls' traditional interests. Childcare, hairdressing and beauty were the most popular choices for girls while there was generally a much wider range of engineering and construction options that are typically chosen by boys. While there is no formal barrier excluding girls from particular courses, the issue of gendered aspirations was one that was identified by interviewees as a particular area of concern for girls.

FE college case study

This Midlands college offers two programmes: one for a small number of Year 11 pupils and one for a larger number of Year 10 pupils. The former was funded through the Single Regeneration Budget (SRB) by the Training and Enterprise Council (TEC) while the latter is funded by the LEA. The programme coordinator reported that approximately one third of programme participants are girls.

Year 11 provision

This programme, which has been offered for the last four years, provides full time education for disaffected Year 11 pupils. In 2000–1 the college was contracted by the TEC to provide 26 places. Most pupils have not been formally excluded but many have self-excluded. The programme aims to re-engage students in education. Pupils are referred to the programme by schools, the LEA behaviour support service or the education welfare service.

Students are 'in-filled' into existing courses and do not have a dedicated tutor group. Many of them take English, mathematics and information technology at whatever level is appropriate for them. They also undertake vocational courses. A small number of students do GCSEs with the college but most of them work towards Open College Network (OCN) qualifications. Approximately 70 per cent of students take other FE courses the following year while the destinations of the remaining pupils are unknown.

Year 10 provision

This full time programme caters for 120 Year 10 pupils and has been offered for three years. Each school in the area nominates five pupils whom they perceive as being 'at risk' of disaffection. Nominees are usually pupils with learning, behavioural or attendance difficulties.

Pupils are taught in discrete groups of fifteen on the college site. The LEA provides the staff for the more academic parts of the programme (English, mathematics, science) and the college provides the information technology, physical education and vocational components of the course. Pupils have work experience placements for two days each week. This part of the programme is organised by the Careers Service. Records indicate that at least 90 per cent of these pupils are maintained in some sort of educational provision the following year. This is usually a return to school or a further college placement. A small number of pupils are referred back to their schools because of attendance or behavioural issues.

Review of education facilities for schoolgirl mothers

A total of 47 units were identified in England from Department of Health data. Thirty of these offered provision for young women up to the age of 16; two for those aged up to 17; six for those aged up to 18 and the remainder for those aged up to 25 years.

Of these units, ten appear to offer full time education, with the remainder specifying a range of provision from five hours a week to morning only or four days a week. Twenty-six offer a crèche or some type of childcare facility. The majority of referrals to these facilities come from schools or education departments, with the remainder coming from social services departments.

Case study: Bristol Unit for schoolgirl mothers

The unit for schoolgirl mothers, which is funded by the LEA, provides education, advice and support to around fifty pregnant girls or schoolgirl mothers a year. The programme follows the National Curriculum, with provision ranging from full time education at the unit to home tuition. Most girls take five GCSEs but also have vocational options. The unit is subject to Ofsted inspections.

At the time of interview, there were 17 girls expected for the 2000–1 academic year. Girls are offered a place once they have opted to keep their child. During the school day, those with babies can leave them in the nursery. At lunch time, the staff and girls eat together and the girls then care for their babies. Transport to and from the unit is provided by taxi. The average length of stay is from one year to fifteen months. Unit staff members then assist students in finding a college placement and in organising childcare.

Particular issues for these girls highlighted by the head of unit included lack of support from their families, lack of affordable childcare that would allow them to study or work and the need for better services from sexual health clinics. As she pointed out: 'There is a need for better provision by sexual health clinics as second pregnancies are a big issue. Bristol has the third worst waiting time for a termination.'

It is interesting to note that most of the girls were never formally excluded from school. Most of them, however, were poor attenders. This is often accentuated when the girl becomes pregnant although, on joining the unit, attendance usually improves.

Case studies of special projects

The following case studies present examples of projects for specific groups of disaffected students that address the needs of young women. (Contact details of project providers can be found in Appendix Three.) The section concludes with a brief summary of some non-gender-specific projects identified in the course of the research representing other styles of working that could be targeted specifically at girls.

The range of approaches includes:

- targeted, time-limited programmes of in-school support;
- open access drop-in support group available during the school lunch break;
- outreach work in schools, with a long-term psychotherapeutic emphasis;
- part-time support in a specialist non-school centre alongside attendance at school;
- home–school support and learning mentors.

Projects for specific groups of young people

York Bridge Centre – an example of a pupil referral unit (PRU)

York LEA has set up the Bridge Centre that offers a six-week programme for pupils at risk of exclusion in Key Stage 3. The Centre is jointly funded by local schools that in 2000–1 used Standards Funding, with the LEA covering the rest of the costs. The initiative started in Autumn 2000.

Pupils judged to be at risk of exclusion, including those who have had one or several fixed-term exclusions, are referred to the Centre by their schools. The Centre has two classes of up to six pupils each. While providing access to the National Curriculum, the programme places a particular emphasis on pupils developing their own learning strategies and on managing their own behaviour.

The Bridge Centre shares an Education Social Worker (ESW) with the Pupil Support Centre who works with individuals, their families and groups of disaffected pupils. There have been only two girls out of the 30 pupils in the four cohorts who had been through the programme at the time of our research. Schools would prefer larger classes in order to be able to send more pupils and make the venture more cost-effective, but the Centre insists that value for money means lower numbers and higher quality.

Outreach – Counselling Service for young Asian women

Outreach is located within the Newham Child and Family Consultation Service and is funded by Social Services Department, the local HAZ and Health Service Trusts. It aims to provide:

■ one-to-one counselling service for young Asian women;
■ information and advice sessions for all young women;
■ mental health promotion amongst young Asian women and in the Asian community;
■ training, consultation and advice to professionals working with young Asian women.

Counselling is available at schools, colleges or at an alternative location of the young woman's choice. The service provides access to counselling and support at a stage when early intervention may prove effective. Young Asian women are being targeted specifically because research has shown that they are three times more likely to attempt suicide or to adopt self-harming behaviours than their white counterparts (Bhui in Johnson and others, 1997). In order to provide a culturally appropriate service, all staff members at Outreach are Asian women.

Special projects for girls

The Positively Girls Course

This project, housed in a Birmingham PRU, was in a pilot stage. From Autumn 1999 to Spring 2001 Birmingham LEA experienced an increase in the numbers of girls excluded from school. The course seeks to tackle this trend. The LEA recognises that girls are under-represented in other provision for young people excluded from school.

Funded from within the existing LEA budget for behaviour support, the Positively Girls Course offers a four-week programme for six girls at a time, working on issues such as self-esteem and self-presentation by in-school support workers. The course is currently open to girls at Key Stage 3 who have to be referred by their in-school support worker. Initial reports indicate that the pilot is working well and it is hoped that the course will be expanded if funds permit.

A-Space

A-Space is based in a large secondary school in Hackney, London. It was set up in 1997 with the aim of providing integrated out-of-school provision and childcare. Young people are engaged as active participants in all aspects of the project's development. It has received its initial funding from a charitable trust but now New Opportunities Funding (NOF) and EAZ funding have also been secured.

A-Space works with 8-14 year olds and addresses health and well-being, as well as providing a programme of other educational and recreational activities. Preventive family support work is also offered by a multidisciplinary team of core and sessional workers who have pioneered many of the policies and practices identified by the DfES under the heading 'study support'.

Since 1998, A-Space has offered a girls' drop-in service once a week at lunch time and an after-school group specifically for girls who use the drop-in. On average, 10 to 15 Year 7 and 8 girls use it each week. The group is run by the A-Space Home-School Link worker and a senior development worker and has proved to be a great success – not least by providing some 'girls-only' space in a school where most of the pupils are boys. It allows the girls to feel more at ease discussing any worries or concerns. In addition, A-Space staff are now offering an in-school support programme run in four-week blocks for eight young people at a time, drawn from Years 7 and 8. This provides help with issues such as isolation, bullying and anger.

UK Youth

UK Youth is a national umbrella group for youth organisations across the country. It is engaged in the Body, Mind and Society programme, which targets young women identified as having a particularly low level of self-esteem. It has also participated in a DfEE programme to promote peer literacy. Both projects were developed in partnership with schools, with the latter now operating in four areas of the country.

The projects run under the Body, Mind and Society programme offer a range of support including art and drama and activities to stimulate discussion. Some support has been offered on a closed group basis in order to foster trust and confidence within the group. The projects reflect the interests and needs of the particular girls attending and also the skills of the youth workers. Interest in the Body, Mind and Society projects has been strong, with a good uptake by the girls invited to participate and positive feedback from their schools.

Examples of other styles of support

Outreach work in schools, with a long-term therapeutic emphasis is offered by the Brandon Centre in London. Established for over thirty years, the Centre offers counselling, psychotherapy and contraceptive services for young people and is funded by charitable funds, the Department of Health, local social services and the local health authority. Therapists work in schools on an individual basis with young people who have been identified as being at risk of exclusion because of behavioural difficulties. The project has worked with girls but focuses mainly on boys because 'they are least able to access psychotherapy'. The length of involvement varies but can be up to three years.

Learning mentor provision is an example of support offered through the East London Schools School-Home Support Scheme, a support service for inner city schools. The scheme has developed learning mentor provision to prevent disaffection and to reduce poor attendance and exclusions. Mentors offer one-to-one work or group support on issues of self-esteem, under-achievement and behavioural problems. The nature and extent of work offered by the mentors is left to individual headteachers to determine. The East London Schools Fund provides a learning mentor coordinator and back-up advice and support. One mentor suggested that this form of support has been welcomed by children and has proved effective in improving communication and in dealing with difficulties at an early stage.

Support in schools alongside provision in a specialist non-school centre is provided by Kids' Company. It is funded with money from local businesses and charitable trusts and takes place in twelve schools across London. Initiatives include playground supervision (structured games), lunch time club, classroom assistance (for specific children and for the whole class) and one-to-one counselling and therapy. The Children's Centre offers out-of-school children full time education based on the National Curriculum. A range of arts and sports activities is also offered for a maximum of 200 children after school. Homework help is also available. The staff–children ratio is high, with support being provided by a range of education professionals. Wherever possible and appropriate, Kids' Company works to support re-integration back into school. Some former pupils attend the homework club and some follow a part-time programme based on an individual behaviour plan as part of their re-integration into the mainstream.

School-based clubs offering targeted support are run by The National Pyramid Trust, a registered charity responsible for running 22 schemes operating in 87 schools. Inter-agency work is a high priority. Some funding has come from the Department of Health and from the National Lottery. The focus is on Year 3 (seven- to eight-year-olds) since it is believed that, at this age, children tend both to want and accept help when they are in need. The selection process usually identifies ten children in an average class of 30, who are likely to benefit from the club. Although all children are offered help, there is a focus on those who are withdrawn and isolated rather than those who are disruptive. The emphasis is on individualised support to the child to develop self-esteem and social skills. Families are involved from the beginning. Research and evaluation of The National Pyramid Trust clubs have indicated that those who have attended a Pyramid group tend to have better social skills and better relationships with peers and adults (Fitzherbert, 1997; Makins, 1997).

7. Conclusions and recommendations

Key findings of the research

A special feature of this research is that it draws on girls' own perceptions of school life and of the use of exclusion in its various forms, both official and unofficial. The interviews with both girls and a wide range of service providers, drawn from education, health, social services and voluntary sector agencies, reveal a complex picture of young women's needs. The research addresses the specific needs of girls and young women. It examines alternative educational provision, focusing on girls' access to and their experiences in such schemes. The research highlights what is working well but it also identifies gaps in provision, as well as arrangements which are either unsuitable for girls or are not being used by them.

Although around 1,800 girls were permanently excluded from school in 1998–9, official statistics disguise the extent of the problem. While girls account for just one in five of the students permanently excluded from secondary school, they are particularly vulnerable to other forms of exclusion. Many young women feel excluded from the processes of education at a particular time; at other times and in different contexts, they will experience greater inclusion. Exclusion can be the result of disciplinary procedures, but it can also occur through feelings of isolation, unresolved personal, family or emotional problems, bullying, emotional withdrawal or truancy. These experiences may be as significant as formal disciplinary exclusion processes if they deny or restrict an individual's access to education and lead to more general social exclusion. As we have said, individual students are not simply in one of two camps, that is to say, either excluded or included. Exclusion and inclusion should be seen as part of a continuum and an individual may move along that continuum at different points in her school career.

Girls are not a priority in schools' thinking about the problems of behaviour management and school exclusion. Throughout the study, a typical response was that girls were 'not a problem'. Such a viewpoint was also evident in many LEAs and other provider agencies. Only by exploring a little deeper did quite widespread problems and concerns start to emerge. However, even then, these were often overshadowed by the difficulties of managing the much greater numbers of boys presenting overtly challenging behaviour.

The 'invisibility' of girls' difficulties has serious consequences in terms of their ability to access help. Since the problem of exclusion amongst girls is seen as so small in comparison to boys, resources are targeted at the latter. This may be exacerbated by a link between criminality and boys' exclusion from school. It may also be the result of the widespread perception that girls are doing well academically in school in comparison to boys. It is not only a lack of resources targeted at girls which constitutes a barrier to them accessing help – the nature of what is on offer and girls' own responses when in difficulty can result in them not receiving help.

The nature of help on offer assumes that provision is equally available for both boys and girls. The findings of this study challenge this assumption. Whilst the research identifies a diverse range of strategies to promote school inclusion, including greater use of the FE sector, provision is largely dominated by boys. As a consequence, not only do many girls feel unwilling to take up the help but many providers do not refer girls since they feel that the provision will be inappropriate given the gender imbalance. This results in further male over-representation and makes it even more unlikely that girls will access support.

Girls' responsiveness to sources of help feeds into this complicated cycle still further, with a widespread view among professionals that a number of girls are defensive, resistant to help and tend to adopt coping strategies which involve a sense of 'escape' or 'withdrawal'.

Identification of girls' needs and the subsequent provision of services are over-compartmentalised. This results in needs being met by separate agencies without necessary links being made. This applies particularly to girls who are pregnant or who have other health or childcare needs. Poor coordination of services is a major concern and can leave girls at risk of no one assuming responsibility for their support.

The use of truancy, self-exclusion and internal exclusion was reported by many of the girls in our sample. Some girls suggested that truancy is a sensible way of dealing with difficulties in school. These unofficial forms of exclusion mean that official statistics are likely to under-estimate the amount of school being missed by girls. This raises concerns about the amount of time girls are missing from school and their lack of a right of appeal when such unofficial exclusions take place.

Gender appears to be an important influence on decisions formally to exclude a young person. Many of the girls in the study expressed the view that the use of exclusion appears arbitrary and lacks consistency. Some suggested that girls could 'get away with more' than their male peers, while others suggested that teachers expect boys to behave badly and were therefore stricter and more exacting in their attitudes towards girls who misbehaved. Professionals also reported these differences in the way boys and girls are disciplined.

Bullying is a serious problem and appears to be a significant factor contributing to girls' decisions to self-exclude. Furthermore, differences in bullying behaviour on the basis of gender mean that bullying amongst girls is not easily recognised. As a result, there is often an institutional failure to tackle bullying among girls effectively. Whilst girls highlight bullying as a serious issue facing them in school, the matter is given a lower priority by the professionals who were interviewed.

Recommendations

These recommendations are based on what the research team learned from interviews with girls and young women of secondary school age, their parents and those professionals who are working with them and their families. In making these recommendations, the researchers are particularly conscious of the need for early intervention strategies that seek to prevent the exclusion of girls and young women from school.

What schools can do

Schools need to consider how their pastoral support systems are meeting the specific needs of girls. Some girls are subject to exclusion as a disciplinary process, while others may withdraw from learning and experience feelings of exclusion. While some may truant, others may continue to attend school without benefiting fully from the opportunities on offer. The research has revealed how girls' problems often remain hidden in school and how particular concerns, such as bullying and racial harassment by girls, may be particularly difficult for adults to detect. As schools take steps to close the 'gender gap' in attainment between girls and boys, and introduce initiatives to address the needs of under-achieving boys, they will also need to identify and support those girls who are under-achieving.

■ Schools should provide support (for example, a counsellor or school nurse) that can be accessed by students on a self-referral system.

- Clear plans are needed for re-integrating pupils who have been out of school as a result of formal exclusion, truancy, pregnancy, etc.
- Policies and practices that address bullying need to acknowledge the more 'subtle' types of bullying to which girls may be particularly vulnerable.
- Schools need to address racial harassment as a specific form of bullying and to provide training and support for staff and pupils to address this issue.
- Schools should provide support and training to teachers to ensure that they have both the skills to identify students who are experiencing difficulties and sufficient knowledge of sources of support.
- Interventions and support for individuals identified as vulnerable need to be discreet and sensitive as girls and young women are often concerned about peer reactions and reputation.
- Effective student consultation and participation procedures are critical (for example, student councils, involvement in drawing up codes of conduct, policy development, etc.) and need to be sensitive to the differing needs of girls and boys.
- Specific initiatives to support girls need to recognise differences in needs between girls, related, for example, to ethnicity, sexuality, maturity and out-of-school responsibilities.
- Access to support systems, alternative curricular arrangements and other opportunities should be monitored by gender and ethnicity.

What providers of alternative education can do

The research team found that, with the exception of specific schemes to meet the needs of pregnant school-age girls and young mothers, providers tend to offer alternative education that is, in principle, open to both girls and boys, but which in practice caters more for boys. There appears to be very little monitoring of the students referred to alternative education schemes, either by gender or ethnicity. This appears to be the case whether the provision is publicly funded (for example, pupil referral units, special schools and further education college places for under-16s), or where voluntary organisations are the providers. Arrangements worked best where colleges and other providers had clear procedures for liaising with schools and LEAs. However, the quality of communication between alternative providers and schools or LEAs was variable.

Most of the alternative provision appears to have been planned with boys in mind. Indeed, one of the key research findings is that many professionals report initially that girls are 'not a problem'. It is only when the issue is explored in more depth that professionals tend to acknowledge that many girls are effectively excluded from learning. Some professionals report that the alternative provision available is often unsuitable for girls. Others are reluctant to send vulnerable girls to schemes that are dominated by boys. One outcome is to increase the imbalance of provision in favour of boys. There are a number of measures that providers might take to improve this situation. Providers of alternative education should:

- monitor the uptake of alternatives and their outcomes by both gender and ethnicity;.
- consider offering some schemes exclusively for girls;
- consult with user-groups, that is, girls and young women, about their particular needs;
- liaise more effectively with schools so that girls can move more easily between mainstream and alternative provision;
- ensure that provision is evaluated and results are made available to other interested parties.

What local authorities can do

The research has revealed that, with an emphasis on boys' achievement and on overcoming boys' disaffection, many professionals are overlooking the needs of girls who are excluded from school or who are vulnerable to exclusion. Local education authorities can play a key role in putting girls' needs back on the agenda. Although there is an increased emphasis on inter-agency working, it is clear from the research that there needs to be further developments in this field if schools and other agencies are to work most effectively on behalf of excluded young people and those who are vulnerable to exclusion.

When schools refer an individual for help, they may find it difficult to assess which agency they should contact, because the young person's needs are complex. Sometimes an individual may be referred to several agencies at once in the hope that one may have the resources to respond quickly. Such arrangements mean that an individual girl may find her needs over-compartmentalised, with no one able to assess the whole picture.

There is an urgent need for local authorities to develop systems, for example, multidisciplinary teams attached to schools, to meet the needs of vulnerable young people. Evidence from this research suggests that professionals believe such teams are beginning to work, although users, including the young people themselves and their parents, are not yet seeing the full benefits of this way of working. Even within a local education authority, it is sometimes proving difficult to coordinate efforts. When a range of other agencies is involved, such as health or social services, then the difficulties are multiplied.

- LEAs should provide commentaries for schools on their exclusion statistics, monitored by gender and ethnicity, which highlight girls' needs even when they form a small proportion of those formally excluded.
- LEAs might helpfully provide a directory of services to support schools working with vulnerable young people.
- LEAs might publish examples of good practice in multidisciplinary working.

What government departments can do

The Government's emphasis on boys' achievement and boys' disaffection has led to a neglect among some professionals of girls' needs. Government departments need to redress the balance, recognising the link between exclusion from school and women's levels of education which have an impact on families and on employment prospects. Support for vulnerable girls will help avoid future social exclusion. Government departments should:

- Recognise that exclusion from school, as it affects girls, is much more extensive than official statistics suggest.
- Review the situation of girls excluded from school, recognising that permanent exclusion as a disciplinary measure needs to be considered alongside unofficial forms of school exclusion that can lead to social exclusion.
- Address the particular needs of girls through the inter-departmental ministerial group on exclusions.
- Require providers accessing government funding to monitor access and outcomes by ethnicity and gender.
- Commission research on further education provision for under-16s, evaluating the outcomes for girls and boys separately.
- Commission further research on the relationship between school exclusion and social exclusion for girls.

Appendix 1:
Study design and methodology

The study is an in-depth, largely qualitative piece of research based on three local education authorities and three education action zones in England. The practical aim of the research is to enhance the awareness and understanding amongst provider agencies, including LEAs, health and social service departments, of the challenges and difficulties which some girls face in school and which lead to disaffection and exclusion in some form. Such knowledge is crucial if effective support strategies for girls at school are to be developed.

Raising the profile of girls' needs and giving them a voice in the process has been a key objective. The following data was collected and analysed from each of the sample areas:

- *Information from a total of 81 girls of secondary school age* was collected via focus group and individual interviews; these meetings took place on school premises. Focus groups typically comprised six girls; some groups were drawn from several year groups, although in a number of schools the group was from a single year group. The sample included girls who were not causing concern in school, those who were at risk of exclusion and some who had experienced exclusion in the past. Attempts were made to ensure the participation of girls looked after by local authorities. Schools were asked to ensure that groups broadly reflected the ethnic make-up of the school. Ten parents whose daughters had experienced difficulties in school including exclusion were also interviewed regarding their views about the support offered to their child. No boys were interviewed.

- *Information from a range of staff working in each of the six areas.* Fifty-five face-to-face interviews took place with a range of service providers across the six areas. Interviewees included staff in mainstream schools, pupil referral units (PRUs), educational psychology and education welfare services, behaviour support teams and education facilities for schoolgirl mothers. Several youth workers and a children's rights officer were interviewed. For each of the six areas, contact was also made with staff working in the local social services department, in particular the personnel responsible for any Quality Protects initiatives, personnel working for Connexions and those working in Youth Offending Teams (YOTS). Contact was also made with local health professionals, including those working in Child and Adolescent Mental Health Services (CAMHS) and voluntary sector organisations. Where face-to-face interviews could not be undertaken, the research team used telephone interviews or postal questionnaire.

■ *A review of relevant research and literature from government, academics and organisations was undertaken.* Documentary evidence such as EAZ Action Plans, LEA Education Development Plans and Social Services Children's Services Plans was also analysed.

The study also included telephone and e-mail surveys:

■ A random selection of 20 further education (FE) colleges across England were contacted by telephone to establish provision for disaffected under-16-year-olds. Colleges were identified from a national list provided by the Further Education Funding Council (FEFC). Data was subsequently collected by telephone interview and supplemented by documents from the colleges. Several colleges in the six sample areas were also visited by the research team.

■ A random selection of units providing education and care for pregnant teenagers and teenage mothers were contacted to investigate the nature of provision offered. These were identified from a Department of Health listing of national education facilities. Two units were visited: one being located in one of the sample areas and the other being randomly selected from those who responded to initial requests for information.

■ All Education Action Zones (EAZs) and ten Health Action Zones (HAZs) were asked to provide information on their activities to promote school inclusion and prevent school exclusion.

■ A range of special projects offering support and therapeutic input for groups of young people either experiencing difficulties in school or with specific needs was identified by various means. These included the placing of adverts in specialist education and child mental health journals and newsletters, including the Internet *Focus Noticeboard* of the Royal College of Psychiatrists.

Selection of sample areas

The six areas were chosen to reflect a geographic spread across England, encompassing both the north and south of the country, rural and urban areas and also areas of high and low levels of economic deprivation.

Sample area 1 is a local education authority in the north of England. The area is predominantly white and is reasonably prosperous. It is significant in the organisational structure of this area that many of the different services that work with children and families are based either in one location or in close proximity to one another. There is also a low turnover of staff. Both of these factors contribute to a high level of inter-agency knowledge and cooperation. Rates of permanent exclusion from school are generally low.

Sample area 2 is an Education Action Zone located in a unitary authority in the south east of England. The area is predominantly white and, whilst prosperous in some areas, there are sizeable areas of high socio-economic deprivation. Within the EAZ action plan there are objectives to ensure the effective transition of pupils across key stages and to promote community involvement in supporting pupils. A specified area of work is to improve pupil motivation and participation through the use of information and communication technology (ICT). Pilot work has also been undertaken to develop a collaborative model of working between school staff and specialist agencies. Education services appear to be subject to regular staff turnover, which is impeding the achievement of some zone objectives.

Sample area 3 is an Education Action Zone located in inner London. It includes two large secondary schools as well as a number of primary schools. A Health Action Zone also covers part of the area. The zone includes a significant number of people from African-Caribbean and refugee communities. The level of socio-economic deprivation is high. EAZ objectives are focused on raising levels of attainment and supporting literacy and numeracy in the primary sector. The EAZ is also addressing 'significant difficulties' with staff recruitment and retention. Schools in the EAZ face considerable challenges and one is in special measures.

Sample area 4 is an Education Action Zone located within a Midlands unitary authority. The EAZ includes 26 schools: three secondary schools, 20 primary schools and three special schools. Poverty and unemployment are high in the zone. The area is predominantly white and there have been concerns about racial harassment of black and minority ethnic people. The EAZ action plan is comprised of 20 strategic plans aimed at *raising attainment, supporting families and fostering social inclusion* (action plan document). Not only attendance and exclusion rates but also effective management of challenging behaviours have been issues for a significant number of schools in the EAZ, and are therefore specifically targeted within these plans.

Sample area 5 is a large metropolitan LEA located in the Midlands and includes both prosperous and socially deprived areas. Approximately 40 per cent of the school population is from minority ethnic communities. At both the strategic planning level and on the ground, there are positive examples of inter-agency and multi-disciplinary working. Across the city there are a wide range of initiatives and projects aimed at supporting children and young people in need. Systematic data gathering about pupils referred to the behaviour support service and exclusions team has been in place for several years and includes the collation of pupil characteristics such as gender, ethnicity, school type, code of practice level and, more recently, public care status.

Sample area 6 is a unitary authority situated in the South. The area is generally prosperous with high levels of employment but some pockets of deprivation. The proportion of the school population from minority ethnic communities is close to the national average. At authority level there is some coordination of services for children with education and children's services coming under a single directorate. A locality mapping exercise looking at indicators of need across a number of life areas (education, social services, health, housing, crime) was undertaken several years ago and has provided useful information that helps with the strategic targeting of resources. The database for children in public care has been expanded and can now provide breakdown by placement, age, ethnicity, gender and educational attainment.

Within each area, the selection of schools took place with the assistance of senior staff working within either the LEA or EAZ. On some occasions, education staff made the first approaches to the schools, PRUs and colleges on behalf of the research team.

Data analysis

Analysis of the interview data was undertaken throughout the study. Individual and focus group interviews were taped and then transcribed. From this, a range of prominent themes were identified. The research team sought to identify any gender-based differences in young people's experiences and any differences on the basis of ethnicity. Our analysis also examined similarities and differences between the perceptions of the girls themselves and professionals working with young people.

Appendix 2:
National policy initiatives

This appendix identifies those government initiatives which interviewees refer to or which fund projects that were investigated.

Standards and Effectiveness Unit

The DfES Standards and Effectiveness Unit (SEU) was formed in 1997. The Unit's key tasks include:

- improving and sustaining standards of attainment of all pupils;
- promoting diversity and innovation;
- monitoring performance and intervening where necessary.

Children's Fund and the Children and Young People's Unit

Launched in November 2000, with funding of £450 million over three years, the aim of this initiative is to tackle child poverty and social exclusion. The Fund will be managed by the Children and Young People's Unit and will have a focus on preventive work for 5–13-year-olds and their families. A key element of the Fund will be the channelling of money directly to local voluntary sector projects.

The new Children's and Young People's Unit workload will include:
- mentoring schemes;
- counselling and advice services;
- parent education on issues such as listening to children and resolving conflict;
- out-of-school activities, including summer schools.

In January 2001, 40 areas in England were invited to apply for the first wave of funding for preventative services. These areas include those with the highest levels of disadvantage amongst children and young people. The plan is that, by 2004, all areas of England will have access to the fund.

Connexions

This is focused on the 13–19 age group and in many ways, complements the Sure Start Plus programme (see pp. 94-5). Each young person will be offered a personal adviser to help him or her with information, advice and support, and to access specialist services if required. This initiative is at the pilot stage in a range of areas around the country and will be phased in over a three-year period starting in April 2001.

Connexions aims to support a flexible curriculum that engages different young people and leads them to relevant, sought-after qualifications; it will provide outreach, information, advice, support and guidance and will target financial support on those in education. It is proposed that the strategy will pay particular attention to the needs of disadvantaged young people and will track their progress. To implement the strategy, a cross-departmental national unit will be set up, which although based in the DfES, will draw in staff from across government and from outside secondments. Connexions partnerships will be developed at local Learning and Skills council level and local management committees will bring together groupings of local partners for organising delivery (Connexions, 1999).

Devolution of Education Welfare Services

A pilot plan to devolve education welfare services to secondary schools, in particular the employment of truancy officers directly by schools, was announced by the Government in Spring 2000 (DfEE, 2000d). The idea is to examine whether attendance officers based within individual schools can tackle truancy more promptly and effectively.

The plan arose following a process of consultation on the proposals contained in the government strategy document, *Tackling Truancy Together* (DfEE, 1999c). It reflects one of a range of strategies introduced to try and improve attendance. Responsibility for the primary and special school sector education welfare services and for pupil referral units remains with the LEA.

Education Action Zones (EAZs)

Introduced in 1998, three waves of EAZs are now in operation, each bringing together a partnership of parents, schools, businesses and LEAs, with the aim being to find innovative ways of raising standards in clusters of schools – typically up to three secondary schools with their associated primaries and special education provision. EAZs have generally been set up in particularly challenging urban or rural areas where there are high levels of socio-economic deprivation.

With regard to promoting school inclusion and reducing exclusions from school, a review of the action plans of second-wave EAZs reveals a mixed picture. Some identify targets to reduce exclusions, but literacy and numeracy targets are a main focus of attention. Much EAZ activity also appears to be taking place in the primary sector. Nevertheless, some interesting examples of innovative work to develop in-school support emerged from this research. For example, some EAZs have developed in-school buddies and learning mentors, whilst others have established nurture groups and home–school liaison officers.

Excellence in Cities

This initiative has a focus on improving inner city education and seeks to 'create a new culture of opportunity and success' (DfEE, 1999d). It is concentrated on six large conurbations and proposals include:

- expanding and recasting the specialist and beacon school programmes;
- extending opportunities for gifted and talented children;
- launching a new network of learning centres.

The strategy aims to tackle disruption in schools by ensuring that every school has access to a learning support unit and to provide a 'learning mentor' for every young person who needs one.

Health Action Zones (HAZs)

Created in 1998, Health Action Zones are responsible for developing new ways of improving health services and tackling inequalities in health. They are expected to work on the basis of partnerships at the local level, and have new financial and management structures from local health authorities. Seventy-eight million pounds was committed to the first wave of 11 zones, followed by a further £15 million when the second wave of 15 zones was announced. In some areas, HAZ funding has contributed towards multi-agency initiatives to promote school inclusion through better identification of children's mental health needs and through improved support for looked after young people.

Home Office Crime Reduction programmes

The Home Office is currently evaluating two projects which aim to prevent young people from offending: On Track and Crime Reduction in Secondary Schools (CRISS). Both projects use preventive measures with children (and their families) who might be predisposed to crime or anti-social behaviour.

On Track is a long-term community-based initiative in 24 of the country's most deprived areas. Original funding of £30m over three years came from the Home Office. Funding has now been subsumed into the Children's Fund. It is a multi-agency project based on family therapy, parenting programmes, home–school partnerships and home visits for families where children are at risk of developing anti-social behaviour. CRISS is a secondary school project that addresses the impact of bullying, truancy, academic achievement, management of offending behaviour and school exclusions on young people's behaviour.

The Home Office acknowledges that, in the past, research into the causes of offending behaviour in children and teenagers was concentrated on boys and that there is now also a need to analyse girls' and young women's behaviour. Both projects will research girls' and young women's anti-social and criminal behaviour, analyse the risk and protective factors for girls and young women and research the anti-social behaviour of girls in specific contexts.

Modernising Mental Health Services – Child and Adolescent Mental Health Services (CAMHS) and Mental Health Innovation Grants

Child and Adolescent Mental Health Services (CAMHS), which work with young people up to the age of 18, have been allocated £84 million modernisation money over three years and £18 million over three years in CAMHS Innovation Mental Health Grant. This money is being used in a wide variety of ways, including the development of in-school support to try to improve the identification of mental health problems in school. Projects address difficulties of a phobic or depressive nature that may result in self-withdrawal.

CAMHS personnel also offer support to project workers engaged in home–school liaison and support work and contribute to a project working to reduce the incidence of mental health problems in temporarily excluded primary and Year 7 children through early intervention. Many projects are being funded on a shared basis using both HAZ and CAMHS money and social services Quality Protects funding.

Quality Protects

This £375 million programme managed by the Department of Health seeks, over three years, to enable local authorities to modernise and improve multi-agency working. The aim is to improve the outcomes for children in need, particularly looked after children. The programme recognises the need to develop an inter-agency strategy for commissioning children's services, including Child and Adolescent Mental Health Services (CAMHS). Under the Quality Protects strategy, a target of 20 days has been set as the maximum time that a looked after young person can be out of education provision. The Department of Health is also due to publish statistics in 2001 which will give the numbers of looked after young people who are permanently excluded from school.

Schools Plus: Building Learning Communities

The remit of this programme emerged from the recommendations of the Social Exclusion Unit's work on neighbourhood renewal, with the aim of the Schools Plus Policy Action Team being:

> to identify the most cost-effective Schools Plus approaches to using schools as a focus for other community services, reducing failure at school, and to develop an action plan with targets to take these forward.
>
> *(DfEE, 2000b)*

Two main areas of activity to raise attainment using Schools Plus activities have been proposed:

- to extend services offered by schools to their pupils;
- greater involvement of the community in the school and the school in the community.

It is also suggested that the programme will build on many of the initiatives already underway such as Excellence in Cities and EAZs.

In extending the services offered by schools, a target is set of providing at least three hours of study support each week for pupils and extending opening hours at some schools. Schools Plus also proposes the development of a Tap-in Programme for both primary and secondary schools. This will offer individual programmes of study and support targeted at pupils at risk of dropping out of education or facing problems of re-integration, due to truancy, exclusion or other long-term absence. Tap-in will also address the needs of refugee children and classes with high pupil turnover.

Single Regeneration Budget (SRB)

SRB grants have helped many schools to purchase equipment and develop a range of out-of-school learning and other activities. Many community-based projects are also based on SRB funding, including those offering support with parenting, adult literacy and education and employment.

SRB began in 1994 and brought together a number of programmes from several government departments, with the aim of simplifying the aid available for regeneration. The priority of SRB funding is to enhance the quality of life for local people in areas of need and to help them to develop the skills and confidence to play a role in the regeneration of their area. It offers support at the local level, often based on partnerships made up of a wide range of local organisations.

Sure Start Plus

Sure Start Plus, announced at the beginning of 2001, builds on the original Sure Start initiative. Sure Start has a general remit for improving and developing services for families with pre-school children and has a budget of £452 million. Sure Start Plus, with a budget of £8 million, focuses specifically on teenage parents aged 17 or under in 15 pilot areas. The pilot areas were selected on the basis of high teenage pregnancy rates and the existence of a local Sure Start programme and a Health Action Zone (HAZ).

Sure Start Plus is part of the Government's national teenage pregnancy strategy and has a specific objective of improving the learning of teenage mothers and fathers and their children. Service recipients will be offered a Sure Start Plus adviser who will work with them to draw up an individual support package covering healthcare, education, employment, childcare, housing and benefits. As a part of this strategy, teenage fathers will be targeted for support in order to help them play a role in their children's upbringing. In addition to providing personal support, the intention is that the initiative will look at existing services to make them more user-friendly and effective for teenagers, especially those who are pregnant.

Appendix 3:
Special projects glossary

A-Space
Lyn French
A-Space
Kingsland School
Shacklewell Lane
London E8 2EY
Tel: 020 7254 4034
email: aspace@tinyonline.co.uk

Brandon Centre
Geoffrey Baruch
Director
Brandon Centre for Counselling and
Psychotherapy for Young People
26 Prince of Wales Road
London NW5 3LG
Tel: 020 7267 4792
email: Gbaruch@compuserve.com

Bristol Unit for Schoolgirl Mothers
Carol Bowery
The Meriton
Meriton Street
St Philips
Bristol BS2 0SU

East London Schools Fund
Amelia Howard
Director
East London Schools Fund
Unit 6
Bow Business Exchange
5 Yeo Street
London E3 3QP
Tel: 020 7538 3479
email:
mail@schoolhomesupportservice.org.uk

Kids' Company
Camilla Batminghelidjh
Kids' Company
Arch 259, Grosvenor Court
Grosvenor Terrace
London SE5 0NP
Tel: 020 7703 5575

National Pyramid Trust
Alan Watson
Chief Executive
84 Uxbridge Road
London W13 8RA
Tel: 020 8579 5108
email: enquiries@nptrust.org.uk

**Outreach Counselling Service for
Young Women**
Farzana Ahmed
OCS
Child and Family Consultation Service
York House
409-11 Barking Road
London E13 8AL
Tel: 020 7445 7847/7848

Positively Girls
Lise Albert
Head of Centre
Oakdale Centre
Umberslade Road
Selly Oak
Birmingham B29 7SB
Tel: 0121 472 7260

UK Youth
Carola Adams
Youthwork, Information and Resources
Manager
UK Youth
2nd Floor Kirby House
20-4 Kirby Street
London EC1N 8TS
Tel: 020 7242 4045
email: info@ukyouth.org

York Bridge Centre
Mrs J Baxter
Headteacher
The Bridge Centre
Fulford Cross
Fulford Road
York YO10 4PB
Tel: 01904 466 860
email: thebridgecentre@talk21.com

Appendix 4:
Key statistics about exclusions and absences from school

'Every day, around 400,000 (5 per cent) pupils are not in school …'
- at least 40,000 are absent without school permission;
- 3,000 are in short, fixed-term exclusions;
- around 6,000 have been, or are being, permanently excluded.'

Audit Commission, 1999b

There are twelve times more fixed-period than permanent exclusions (Audit Commission, 1999b).

In the early 1990s, the number of exclusions rose most rapidly in primary schools (Smith, 1998).

Between 1991–6, the annual rate of pupils permanently excluded from state schools in England increased by approximately 400 per cent (Cooper and others, 2000).

The number of recorded permanent exclusions decreased from 12,300 in 1997–8 to 10,500 in 1998–9. This represents a drop from 0.17 per cent of the school population to 0.14 per cent. Almost 80 per cent of permanent exclusions were pupils aged 12-15 (DfEE, 2000a).

The most recent Ofsted report notes that 'despite the overall falls in exclusion nationally, minority ethnic pupils, particularly Black Caribbean boys and boys of mixed heritage, continue to be excluded disproportionately' (Ofsted, 2001).

1997 DfEE figures indicated that African-Caribbean pupils were excluded at a rate almost five times that which could be expected from their number in the general school population (Smith, 1998).

Recent figures from the Department of Health reveal that 500 young people looked after by local authorities in England were permanently excluded from school in the year ending 30 September 2000; this equates to 1.5 per cent of the total number of looked after young people in that time period (DoH, 2001b).

Only 18.5 per cent of those excluded from secondary school ever go back to mainstream education (Parsons, 1996a).

There are strong links between not attending school and involvement in criminal behaviour – research in 1996 found that 65 per cent of school-age offenders sentenced in court were non-attenders or had been excluded from school (Audit Commission, 1996).

An anonymised survey of 35,000 pupils in Years 10 and 11 reported that 30 per cent of those who responded said they had truanted at least once in the previous half term; many had engaged in 'post-registration truancy'; 'the study had an 83 per cent response rate: it is likely that many of those who did not respond were truanting at the time of the survey' (Social Exclusion Unit, 1998, p.4).

Rates for inner city truancy are 33 per cent higher than the national figure (DfEE, 1999c).

Exclusion from school results in considerable costs – replacement education costs approximately twice as much as standard mainstream education; over 20 per cent of permanently excluded pupils use social services and a little over a quarter incur a cost to the police (Parsons, 1996a).

References

Advisory Centre for Education (1993) *Children out of School: A guide for parents and schools on non-attendance at school.* ACE

Ainscow, M, Farrell, P, Tweddle, D and Malki, G (1999) *Effective Practice in Inclusion and in Special and Mainstream Schools Working Together.* DfEE

Atkinson, M, Halsey, K, Wilkin, A and Kinder, K (2000) *Raising Attendance 2: A detailed study of education welfare working practice.* National Foundation for Educational Research

Audit Commission (1996) *Misspent Youth.* Audit Commission

Audit Commission (1999a) *Children in Mind: Child and adolescent mental health services.* Audit Commission

Audit Commission (1999b) *Missing Out: LEA management of school attendance and exclusion.* Audit Commission

Ball, M (1998) *School Inclusion: The school, the family and the community.* Joseph Rowntree Foundation

Buchanan, A and Hudson, B (2000) *Promoting Children's Emotional Well-being: Messages from research.* Oxford University Press

Children's Society (1999) *Principles of Policy and Good Practice to Promote School Inclusion.* The Children's Society

Connexions (1999) *Connexions: The best start in life for every young person.* Connexions Service National Unit

Cooper, P, Drummond, M, Hart, S, Lovey, J and McLaughlin, C (2000) *Positive Alternatives to Exclusion.* Routledge/Falmer

Crozier, J and Anstiss, J (1995) Out of the spotlight: Girls' experience of disruption, *in* Lloyd-Smith, M and Dwyfor Davies, J eds *On the Margins: The educational experiences of 'problem' pupils.* Trentham

Cullingford, C (1999) *The Causes of Exclusion: Home, school and the development of young criminals.* Kogan Page

Dearden, C and Becker, S (1998) *Young Carers in the UK.* Carers' National Association and Young Carers' Research Group, Loughborough University

Dennison, C and Coleman, J (2000) *Young People and Gender: A review of research*. A report submitted to: the Women's Unit Cabinet Office and the Family Policy Unit, Home Office, by the Trust for the Study of Adolescence. Women's Unit/Cabinet Office

Department for Education and Employment (1997) 'Permanent Exclusions from School in England 1995-6'. *DfEE News* 342/97, 30 October

Department for Education and Employment (1999a) *Social Inclusion: Pupil Support*. Circular 10/99. DfEE

Department for Education and Employment (1999b) *Social Inclusion: The LEA role in Pupil Support*, Circular 11/99. DfEE

Department for Education and Employment (1999c) *Tackling Truancy Together: A strategy document*. DfEE

Department for Education and Employment (1999d) *Excellence in Cities*. DfEE

Department for Education and Employment (2000a) *Statistics of Education: Permanent exclusions from maintained schools in England*. Issue 10/00. The Stationery Office

Department for Education and Employment (2000b) *Schools Plus: Building learning communities*. DfEE

Department for Education and Employment (2000c) *Guidance on the Education of Children and Young People in Public Care*. DfEE

Department for Education and Employment (2000d) 'Jacqui Smith announces pilot areas for devolving education welfare services to secondary school'. *DfEE News*. DfEE

Department of Health (1999) *The Framework for the Assessment of Children in Need and their Families*. Department of Health

Department of Health Statistical Bulletin (2000a) *Children Looked After by Local Authorities Year Ending 31 March 2000, England and Wales*. Bulletin 2000/15. Department of Health

Department of Health Statistical Bulletin (2000b) *Children on Child Protection Registers 1999–2000*. Department of Health

Department of Health Statistical Bulletin (2000c) *Statistics from the Regional Drug Misuse: Database for six months ending September 2000*. Department of Health

Department of Health Statistical Bulletin (2001a) *Children Accommodated in Secure Units, Year Ending 31 March 2000: England and Wales*. Bulletin 2001/17. Department of Health

Department of Health (2001b) *Outcome Indicators for Looked After Children year ending 30 September 2000, England*. Department of Health

Divert (1999) *Divert Annual Report 1998–1999*. Divert

Epstein, D and Johnson, R (1998) *Schooling Sexualities*. The Open University Press

Fitzherbert, K (1997) Promoting Inclusion: The work of The Pyramid Trust, *The Journal of the Association of Workers for Children with Emotional and Behavioural Difficulties*, 2, 3

Gillborn, D and Gipps, C (1996) *Recent Research on the Achievements of Ethnic Minority Pupils*. HMSO

Gillborn, D (1995) *Racism and Antiracism in Real Schools*. The Open University Press

Gillborn, D (1998) 'Exclusion from school: An overview of the issues', *in* Donovan, N *ed*, *Second Chances, 11–18*. New Policy Institute

Hayden, C (1997) *Children Excluded from Primary School: Debates, evidence, responses*. The Open University Press

Hayden, C and Dunne, S (2001) *Outside, Looking In: Children and families' experience of school exclusion*. Advisory Centre for Education/The Children's Society

Hey, V (1997) *The Company She Keeps: An ethnography of girls' friendships*. Open University Press

House of Commons Education and Employment Select Committee (1998) *Disaffected Children*, Fifth Report, Volume 1. The Stationery Office

Include (2000) *'This time I'll stay' – re-integrating young people permanently excluded from school*. Include

Johnson, S, Ramsey, R, Thornicroft, G, Brooks, L, Lelliott, P, Pack, E, Smith, H, Chisholm, D, Audini, B, Knapp, M and Goldberg, D (1997) *London's Mental Health*. King's Fund

Katz, A, Buchanan, A, and Bream, V (2001) *Bullying in Britain – Testimonies from teenagers*. Young Voice

Kinder, K, Harland, J, Wilkin, A and Wakefield, A (1995) *Three to Remember: Strategies for disaffected pupils*. National Foundation for Educational Research

Kinder, K, Wakefield, A, Wilkin, A (1996) *Talking Back — Pupil views on disaffection*. National Foundation for Educational Research

Kinder, K, Kendall, S, Downing, D, Atkinson, M, Hogarth, S (1998) *Raising Behaviour: Nil Exclusion? Policy and Practice*. National Foundation for Educational Research

Kurtz, Z and Thornes, R (2000) *Health Needs of School Age Children*. DfEE and Department of Health

Labour Force Survey Autumn Quarter (2000). Office for National Statistics Autumn Quarter (Analysis by DfES Analytical Services)

Lloyd, G and O'Regan, A (1999) Education for social exclusion? Issues to do with the effectiveness of educational provision for young women with 'social, emotional and behavioural difficulties', *Emotional and Behavioural Difficulties*, 4, 2, 38-46

Lloyd, G (2000) 'Gender and exclusion from school', *in* Salisbury, J and Riddell, S *eds Gender, Policy and Educational Change*. Routledge

Macpherson, W and others (1999) *The Stephen Lawrence Inquiry*. The Stationery Office

Madge, N, Burton, S, Howell, S and Hearn, B (2000) *9 to 13: The Forgotten Years?* National Children's Bureau

Makins, V (1997) *The Invisible Children: Nipping failure in the bud*. David Fulton

Mayet, G (1993) Exclusions and schools, *Multicultural Education Review*, 15, 7-9

Meltzer, H, Gatward, R, Goodman, R and Ford, T (2000) *The Mental Health of Children and Adolescents in Great Britain, Summary Report*. Office for National Statistics

Meltzer, H, Harrington, R, Goodman, R and Jenkins, R (2001) *Children and Adolescents who Try to Harm, Hurt or Kill Themselves*. Office for National Statistics

Mental Health Foundation (1999) *The Fundamental Facts*. Mental Health Foundation

Miller, P (1995) 'Review of truancy in English secondary schools' *in* O'Keefe, D and Stoll, P *eds Issues in School Attendance and Truancy*, 3-7. Pitman

Milner, J *eds Exclusion from School: Interprofessional issues for policy and practice.* Routledge

Morris, M, Nelson, J, and Stoney, S (1999) *Disadvantaged Youth: A critical review of the literature on scope, strategies and solutions*, DfEE Research Brief no 169. DfEE

Munn, P, Lloyd, G and Cullen, M (2000) *Alternatives to Exclusion from School*. Paul Chapman

Nehaul, K (1996) *The Schooling of Children of Caribbean Heritage*. Trentham

Normington, J (1996) Exclusion from school: the role of outside agencies *in* Blythe, E and

Norwich, B (1994) *Segregation and Inclusion: English LEA statistics 1988-92*. Centre for Studies on Inclusive Education

Office for Standards in Education (1996) *Exclusions from Secondary Schools 1995-6*. Ofsted

Office for Standards in Education (2000) *The Annual Report of Her Majesty's Chief Inspector of Schools, 1998-9*. The Stationery Office

Office for Standards in Education (2001) *Improving Attendance and Behaviour in Secondary Schools - Strategies to promote educational inclusion*. Ofsted

Osler, A (1997) *Exclusion from School and Racial Equality: Research report*. Commission for Racial Equality

Osler, A and Hill, J (1999) Exclusion from school and racial equality: an examination of government proposals in the light of recent research evidence, *Cambridge Journal of Education*, 29, 1, 33-62

Osler, A (2000) Children's rights, responsibilities and understandings of school discipline, *Research Papers in Education*, 15, 1, 49-69

Osler, A and Osler, C (in press) Inclusion, exclusion and children's rights: a case study of a student with Asperger's Syndrome, *Emotional and Behavioural Difficulties.*

Osler, A, Watling, R and Busher, H (2000) *Reasons for Exclusion from School*, Research Report No 244. DfEE

Parffrey, V (1994) Exclusion: failed children or systems failure? *School Organisation*, 14, 2, 107-20

Parsons, C (1996a) *Exclusion from School: The public cost*. Commission for Racial Equality

Parsons, C (1996b) Permanent exclusions from schools in England in the 1990s: Trends, causes and responses, *Children and Society*, 10, 177-86

Parsons, C and Howlett, K (1995) Difficult dilemmas, *Education*, December, 22-9

Parsons, C and Howlett, K (2000) *Investigating the Re-integration of Permanently Excluded Young People in England.* Include

Pomeroy, E (2000) *Experiencing Exclusion.* Trentham

Reid, K (1999) *Truancy and Schools.* Routledge

Rowbotham, D (1995) Searching for the truth, *Education*, September

Salmon, G, James, A, Cassidy, E, and Javaloyes, M (2000) Bullying. A review: Presentations to an adolescent psychiatric service and within a school for emotionally and behaviourally disturbed children, *Clinical Child Psychology and Psychiatry*, 5, 4, 563-79.

Schools Health Education Unit (2000) *Young People in 1999.* Schools Health Education Unit

Sheppard, C (1997) 'What can agencies outside the education service contribute?' *in* Hayden, C *Children Excluded from Primary School: Debates, evidence and responses.* Open University Press

Smith, R (1998) *No Lessons Learnt: A survey of school exclusions.* The Children's Society

Social Exclusion Unit (1998) *Truancy and School Exclusion.* Cabinet Office

Social Exclusion Unit (1999) *Teenage Pregnancy.* Cabinet Office

Social Exclusion Unit (2001) *Preventing Social Exclusion.* Cabinet Office

Stanley, L and Arora, T (1998) Social exclusion amongst adolescent girls: their self-esteem and coping strategies, *Educational Psychology in Practice*, 14, 2, 94-100

Stirling, M (1994) The end of the line, *Special Children*, 76, 27-9

Street, C (2000) *Whose Crisis? Meeting the needs of children and young people with serious mental health* problems. Young Minds

Vernon, J and Sinclair, R (1998) *Maintaining Children in School: The Contribution of social service departments.* National Children's Bureau

Wilson, P (1996) *Mental Health in Your School.* Jessica Kingsley

Wright, C, Weekes, D and McGlaughlin, A (2000) *'Race', Class and Gender in Exclusion from School.* Falmer

Index